Y0-BRV-428

HOW TO REAP RICHES FROM RAW LAND:

Guide to Profitable Real Estate Speculation

HOW TO REAP RICHES FROM RAW LAND:

Guide to Profitable Real Estate Speculation

Glen Nicely

Prentice-Hall, Inc. Englewood Cliffs, N.J.

Prentice-Hall International, Inc., *London*
Prentice-Hall of Australia, Pty. Ltd., *Sydney*
Prentice-Hall of Canada, Ltd., *Toronto*
Prentice-Hall of India Private Ltd., *New Delhi*
Prentice-Hall of Japan, Inc., *Tokoyo*

Reward Edition . . . . . . July 1978

Library of Congress Cataloging in Publication Data

Nicely, Glen,
How to reap riches from raw land.

1. Real estate investment. 2. Real estate investment—United States. I. Title.
HD1375.N5 332.6'324 73-22282

Printed in the United States of America

WHAT THIS BOOK CAN DO FOR YOU

Two or three times a year I drop in on my old friend George Lewis.

He's now past 80–an age when most men, who are fortunate enough to achieve it, are willing to leave business to another generation.

George is a real estate trader, or speculator, or investor–take your pick of terminology.

Nearly every time I visit him he will describe a recent real estate purchase or sale. If it is a purchase we usually wind up driving to the property and looking it over and invariably he will tell me that he will not purchase any more property, "because at my age I just don't want to be bothered."

Then on the next trip, when I inquire as to whether he has bought or sold any real estate since my last visit, his eyes sparkle and with a wry smile he will say, "I ran into a deal the other day just too good to pass up–but now I am really quitting."

Since George has long since made his first million, I suspect trading real estate has now become a game–but one which he plays hard–and plays to win.

The fact that he doesn't read and can barely sign his name has been no apparent stumbling block.

What could this man have done with a good education? Maybe he would have been a 20th century tycoon or perhaps he would have been a salaried employee for someone else who made a million. Education often makes people feel more secure and sometimes more conservative.

After introducing my friend, I wish I could write this book about his system. I wish I could emulate him and let you in on his secrets.

Unfortunately for you and me, he has no system which I can define—no set pattern—no rules of thumb which guarantees success.

He trades in commercial property, farm property, mountain land, subdivision property—you name it—chances are—he has bought and sold it *for a profit.*

He is one of those rare individuals who has the Midas touch for real estate. If you happen to be another one—reading this book may be a waste of your time.

All of us have encountered those rare and talented individuals in many fields—the man who can beautifully play five different musical instruments but has never had a lesson and cannot read a note. We have known of baseball players—many are legends now—who rose to a pinnacle of fame after joining the major leagues without a prior day's formal coaching in the fundamentals. When discovered on the sandlot or in the bush league they had already developed the grace, poise, style, speed and swing that set them aside from the masses. Then there is the outdoorsman who can train a hunting dog, track a deer, land the big bass and always keep his bearings in a wilderness—a sixth sense, some call it.

Sadly, however, most of us only succeed in endeavors about which we are willing to study and learn the fundamentals—to plan and strive—to fail and start over.

I wish I could tell you, that at an early age, I grasped the full potential of land speculation—equipped myself with a vast amount of knowledge of the field and pursued it in a systematic manner.

The truth of the matter is, the full impact of the potential in real estate speculation only got through to me a few years ago.

I was engaged in land acquisition for housing of low-income families, to be constructed on a turnkey basis by private developers with funding provided by the national government. Initially, I did this work for my own company, then later as a consultant for a larger company to which I sold my firm.

I optioned and purchased more than a million dollars worth of unimproved land. In many instances the profits which the landowners realized were greater than the profits to the developer who took enormous risks and often spent as much as three years on a project.

Further reflection on the matter revealed I had been speculating, in a small rather haphazard way, in raw land for more than twenty years and every transaction had been profitable—with the exception of one small piece of mountain land which I sold to my brother at a loss when I moved to another state—and on which he subsequently made a 200 per cent profit.

Now that I look back, I do not understand why I did not get excited about my first venture which came about many years ago when I was county agricultural agent for a rural county.

I came across a small well located farm, with a new stone house about 90 per cent completed, which had been placed on the market following a domestic litigation. I made an offer and had it accepted. The price was a bargain. I used a great amount of leverage—not by plan or design but out of necessity—since my capital was extremely limited. In less that a year I sold the farm at a profit in excess of my annual wages at the time. This venture should have been enough to get me seriously started on land speculation but I suppose I wrote it off as a freak deal or beginners luck.

Anyway, many years and dozens of profitable transactions later, it finally dawned on me that I had often bought and sold common stocks with about as many "losers" as winners—had played a little poker and bet on a few ball games without amassing any records on which I could brag—or any system which I could recommend to friends—but that real estate speculation, even haphazardly pursued, had been consistently profitable.

Finally I started to plan a program of buying and selling and boning up on the subject by reading numerous books and periodicals on the subject–taking into account my time, my capital, and what I wanted to accomplish. Many raise the question as to how you can plan a program in real estate speculation when you have no way of knowing when you will be able to sell or what price you will receive.

Obviously, your program cannot be laid out with the accuracy and finesse of a man who put his money in government bonds, savings and loan associations, and preferred stocks.

You will often be surprised, however, how many goals you can set and reach if you *plan your work and work your plan.*

A prominent Hollywood actor revealed recently to a nationwide television audience that he made more in one year in real estate than the previous 25 years as an actor.

He explained that he became fascinated after reading a book by a successful trader in real estate and followed up by enrolling in real estate classes at a nearby university where he studied as a part-time student for three years.

Likely, he had more capital with which to work than most of us. However, he needed a knowledge of the business to recognize the opportunities and put his capital to work on a profitable basis.

Much of the wealth of the Astors, one of the nation's most prominent families, was acquired through real estate. The financial patriarch, John Jacob Astor, began setting aside surplus income for buying New York property before 1800 when the city population was 25,000. The 20th century has its share of real estate tycoons. Some have inherited it, some had the foresight, wisdom and energy to earn it, and others got lucky.

But this is not a book about the few who made it real big. This book is for the average individual, already established in a job or profession, who seeks to increase his income–even double or triple it–through the wise use of his surplus capital.

An ambition to be president of the United States or to be very wealthy is laudable, but it can be very frustrating if you calculate the percentages. On the other hand, an ambition to increase your

earnings with which to better educate your children, have great
financial security, or to retire at an early age, is both laudable an
attainable.

A speculator by one definition is one who expects to make
greater than normal return for a greater than normal risk. Th
writer believes that, properly pursued, real estate offers an oppor
tunity for greater than normal profits without taking greater tha
normal risks.

The title notwithstanding–our real subject is *profits.* Specula
tion is the vehicle by which we achieve them.

Some misunderstand and deplore the use of the word *specu
lator.* I use it without apologies believing that the test o
acceptability of any transaction rests not in the terminology
applied to the participants but whether, in achieveing their goals,
they observe the rules of fairness, honesty and ethical responsibility.

Investment is sometimes defined as the outlay of money for
income or profit. Some writers interchange the terms freely and
based on any definition which I have come across, there are some
elements of speculation in any investment and vice versa. For
example, tax shelters discussed at length in this book are usually
referred to as investments but can also be highly speculative.

Since clear cut definitions, which distinctively separate the two,
are hard to come by and in order that the writer and the reader
may stay on the same wave length, I list here a few of the
characteristics of each as used in this book:

Speculator

1. A speculator considers income from property a by product.
2. A speculator expects to own property for a relatively short duration–usually less than five years.
3. A speculator uses greater leverage and less equity than an investor.
4. A speculator often uses options instead of ownership to hold property for appreciation.

5. A speculator usually (but not always) concentrates on unimproved property.
6. A speculator acquires property with the primary aim of reselling for profit.
7. A speculator attempts to buy property in the early stages of transition.
8. A speculator often purchases property on which accurate appraisal, based on comparable sales, would be difficult—relying heavily on his own judgment as to both present and future value.
9. A speculator creates a market in slack times—off years. He helps average out brokerage business—some brokers will admit that 10 to 20 per cent, and sometimes higher amounts, of their sales are made to speculators. In the auction business 50 per cent to 75 per cent of the purchases are by speculators.
10. A speculator is often an idea man. He must be resourceful in arriving at a use for property—often a use never thought of by the owner from whom he purchased it.

Investor

1. An investor is one who contemplates holding property for long duration.
2. An investor deals chiefly in income producing property.
3. An investor usually gets the highest possible monthly or annual return.
4. An investor's aim is usually to pay fully for his property as rapidly as possible—whereas the speculator often expects to sell his equity for a profit.
5. His purpose in acquiring property is sometimes to create an income producing estate for his heirs.
6. An investor usually acquires property with a specific use in mind. The investor's greatest weakness is often in becoming too inflexible. While his risk may be generally less than a

speculator–it may be greater. For example, property held in trust for a long period of time may suffer from a decaying neighborhood and if it is downtown property it is extremely vulnerable to value erosion brought about by sprawling subdivisions followed by large shopping malls.

Knowingly or unknowingly, everyone engages in some speculation, whether it is a farmer planting his crops or any individual who buys a life insurance policy with the sure knowledge that he will ultimately die but speculating with the underwriter as to whether it will be *sooner*–or *later.*

Speculation of this type is incidental rather than the intention. This book is for the individual who *intends* to speculate in real estate.

Those who lack the courage, energy or desire to speculate will be happier to earn regular wages, keep their savings on interest-bearing deposits in life insurance and high grade bonds and rely on savings, social security and the company pension plan for retirement.

If you fall into this category this book is not for you. If, however, you would like to add to your income and start building an estate for later years, and if you have a reasonable amount of courage, some excess energy and enjoy playing the money game–this book can start you on the road to profits with excitement along the way.

If you have often envied your friend who seems to have a knack for real estate deals or "is the luckiest trader I ever saw," keep turning the pages and you can learn in a brief period a lot of the tricks of the trade which may have taken him years to acquire before he got so lucky.

How much money are we talking about?

That is up to you. Perhaps a few hundred or a few thousand extra dollars a year. Maybe doubling your present income.

The interest, time and devotion, and of course the amount of capital which you now have or will acquire will affect your results.

What about luck? Don't knock it, but don't depend on it.

We have all seen examples of someone who inherited a relatively inexpensive piece of farmland, becoming the beneficiary of a major highway interchange and getting wealthy overnight, or the growth pattern of a city suddenly taking off toward the North side–raising the price of land from two or three hundred dollars an acre to several thousand dollars an acre in a span of a few years.

A friend of mine purchased a motel in the edge of a resort village several years ago. On a nearby lot there was a riding stable which attracted flies. The pests were not content to spend all of their time with the horses but often divided their days between the equine at the stables and the Homo sapiens lounging around the motel pool. To stop the annoyance, my friend was forced to purchase the lot for $9,000. The village has mushroomed into a thriving resort city and now the lot is valued at $150,000. This man is an astute real estate trader but he owns this valuable lot today because of horseflies–not foresight.

These breaks do not come to most of us but chances are that you will, at least in a limited way, be the beneficiary of some outside favorable circumstances if you start investing in real estate.

As my fishing partner often reminds me when I stop casting to light my pipe or eat a sandwich, "if you want to catch fish you've got to keep your plug wet." Nothing good can happen to your property if you don't own any.

This book is not a text or reference volume. Its purpose is not to prepare you to pass an examination for a broker's license. It is based largely upon the experiences and observations of the writer and is written with a twofold purpose–namely:

1. To point out the almost limitless opportunities for making profits in real estate.
2. To challenge you to take advantage of these opportunities.

Glen Nicely

CONTENTS

WHAT THIS BOOK CAN DO FOR YOU........................5

Part 1: The Profit Goal–How to Reach It 19

1. THE GREATEST LAND BOOM 21

Rising Prices . Farmland . Home Sites–Industrial Property . Second Homes . Competition from Large Corporations . Multifamily Housing . Foreign Lands Advancing . Holding Land Can Be Expensive

2. LAND AND PEOPLE 26

Land Being Absorbed . Population Densities and the Future . Declining Birthrate . Shifting Uses–More Difficult

Population Trends 28

Rural Population Small–Farm Prices Good . Where One Broker Found a Market . Where People Want to Live . Change in Growth Regions

3. GETTING STARTED 32

Where to Start–Things to Know 32

Brokers Can Be Helpful . Undeveloped Property . Things to Know–Tools to Use . Learn the Fundamentals

Setting Your Goals 39

GETTING STARTED *(Continued)*

Factors Influencing Value
Use Your Own Judgment 41
An Expensive Lesson . Never Look Back . Advice to Take–and Not to Take . Greatest Problem

4. REAL ESTATE VERSUS COMMON STOCKS 46

5. RAW LANDS AND PROFITS 52

Two Properties Compared . Statistics Scarce . How Much Profit Should You Expect? . Use Credit to Increase Returns . Compensation to Expect . Double Your Income . The Four Year Plan

6. WHAT TO BUY 64

Why Buy . The Best Buys (Sleepers) . Bargain Situations . Good Buy–Quick Profit . Another Quick Turnover . My First Venture . The Once in a Lifetime Opportunity . Front End Profit . Selling to a Developer
Cheap Property 70
Demands High Return . "Ground Rules" for Success
Distress Property 71
Leveraging on Distressed Property
Making Profitable Choices 72
Residential Lots . Farmland . Opportunities Summarized
Home Ownership–Wise or Foolish? 74
Advantages of Home Ownership . Home Ownership at an Earlier Age . Housing Costs . The High Costs of Owning . One Example . How to Gain on Your Home Mortgage

7. LEVERAGE 81

Two Good Leverage Deals . Increased Taxes–Owner Panics . Need Income–Not Ready to Sell . More Leverage–More Risk . Leveraging Opportunities Greatest in Real Estate . No Interest Leveraging . Many Option Possibilities . Keep Reserves in Time and Money

8. SUBDIVIDING RESIDENTIAL LAND 86

Reasons for Demand . Factors Affecting Profit . Low Investment–High Return . High Land Costs–Low Return . Some Do's and Don'ts When

SUBDIVIDING RESIDENTIAL LAND *(Continued)*

Subdividing . Easiest to Handle . Buy Tract–Wholesale Subdivision . Leverage Possibilities . How to Proceed . Don't Overdevelop . Other Suggestions . Protective Covenants . Protecting the Environment . Ordering Topo Maps

9. CAVEAT EMPTOR 97

Questions to Be Considered When Buying
Surveying 100
Proper Identification . Watch the Expenses . How to Plot a Deed
Mail Order Land Buying 101
Mrs. Roberts "Wins" a Lot . Misrepresented and Overpriced . Laws Tightened . 13 Miles to Nearest Grocery . Many Will Buy on Easy Terms . Florida–a Paradox . HUD's Experience

10. ACQUISITION AND OWNERSHIP 108

Listing (or Listing Contract) . Offer to Purchase . Title Search . Abstract of Title . Survey . Certificate of Title . Title Insurance . Escrow . Deed . Fee Simple Title . Trust Deed . Closing Statement . Recording Your Deed . Taking Title . Good Records Are Essential

11. ANALYZING AND FORECASTING 120

Federal Reserve System . Employment Trends . Other Indicators . Small Communities Less Affected by Patterns . Every Deal Unique . Growth and Inflation . Growing Economy . Emotional Influences
The Great Depression–Can It Happen Again? 127
Conditions Preceding the Depression . Florida Land Boom . Higher Stock Prices . Worst Yet to Come . Other Land Booms

12. BUYING AND SELLING FARM PROPERTY 133

Quick Profit on Farmland . Knowledge of Farming Important . Farms for Investment . Agricultural Extension Service . Vocational Agricultural Departments . Soil Conservation Service . Agricultural Stabilization and Conservation Service . No Shortage of Farmland . Some Considerations Before Buying
Financing Farm Property 139
Farmers Home Administration . Federal Land Bank . Production Credit Associations

13. BUYING AND SELLING AT AUCTION 144

Suitable Property for Auctions . Types of Auctions . How to Buy at Auction . When the Bidding Starts

14. DEPRECIATION AND TAX SHELTERS 149

Depreciation 149
Economic Obsolescence . Calculating Depreciation . Straight Line Method . Declining Balance . Sum-of-the-Digits
Tax Shelters 152
Benefits Multiplied . Most Favorable Shelters . Current IRS Guidelines . Depreciation Schedule

15. SYNDICATING REAL ESTATE 158

Public Syndication . Real Estate Investment Trusts . Private Syndication . The New Breed–Real Estate Packagers

16. APPRAISING FOR SPECULATION 164

Computing Land Areas

17. FINANCING 169

18. ADVERTISING 173

19. BROKERAGE 175

Licensing Laws . Commissions . Multiple Listings . Net Listings and Open Listings . Pros and Cons of the Brokerage Business

Part II: Higher Use–The Speculators Market 179

20. SINGLE FAMILY RESIDENCES 180

21. APARTMENTS, CONDOMINIUMS AND COOPERATIVES 182

Reasons for More Apartments . Duplex or Fourplex Worth Considering . What Size Project? . Expense/Income Ratio . Supplying the Land .

APARTMENTS, CONDOMINIUMS AND COOPERATIVES *(Continued)*

Swinging Singles . Financing . Condominiums and Cooperatives . Condominiums, Cooperatives–Compared . Advantages Listed by HUD . Condominiums Most Popular . Conventional Financing . HUD Insured Financing . Family Unit Mortgage Limitations

22. SHOPPING CENTERS 191

Real Estate Values Influenced . Cost of Space

23. INDUSTRIAL REAL ESTATE 193

Warehousing 194

Speculative Buildings . How One Speculator Finances Warehouses

Industrial Parks 197

Thorough Planning and Ample Time Essential . Examples of Profits on Industrial Parks . Price of Industrial Land

24. MOBILE HOMES 200

Why Mobiles Sell . Who Uses Mobiles–and Where? . Trends Toward Luxury . Mobiles Have Their Drawbacks . Renting Mobiles . Selling Land for Mobile Homes . Financing Mobile Units

Mobile Home Parks 204

What Size Park? . Density and Income . Financing Mobile Parks . HUD Insured Loans . Good Parks Are Still Needed

25. RECREATION LAND 207

26. INDUSTRIALIZED HOUSING 209

Major Types . Failures Many–Growth Slow . Optimism and Drawbacks

Part III: Heavy Hand in Housing–Government Programs 211

27. HUD–HISTORY AND PROGRAMS 212

HUD Insured Programs . Other HUD Programs . HUD's Influence on Raw Land

Multifamily Subsidy Programs 214

HUD-HISTORY AND PROGRAMS *(Continued)*

Section 236 Program . Numerous Failures
Public Housing for the Low Income 216
Who Qualifies for Public Housing? . How Projects Are Developed . Providing Housing Sites . Leasing Housing
Financing HUD Insured and Subsidized Housing 218
The Federal National Mortgage Association . The Government National Mortgage Association . The Federal Home Loan Bank Board . Federal Home Loan Mortgage Corporation

INDEX 221

HOW TO REAP RICHES FROM RAW LAND:

Guide to Profitable Real Estate Speculation

Part I

The Profit Goal—How to Reach It

1

THE GREATEST LAND BOOM

This nation has witnessed numerous land booms and some people are still around who made and lost fortunes in the big Florida boom and bust of the 1920's.

Most past booms were isolated to regions and were often generated and nurtured by fast buck promoters. None of these compare in size and scope with the greatest land boom the world has experienced which occurred during the 1960's and gathered increasing momentum in the early 1970's.

While some spots are hotter than others, this boom recognizes no boundaries. During the 1960's and early 1970's land has been sought and bought—invested in—and speculated in—by more people than ever before in the world's history.

And while it has its share of touts and promoters, their influence is insignificant in the overall picture. The ever increasing population, the dwindling supply of good land, economic growth and inflation—are the prime motivating forces. While undoubtedly there will be cooling off periods, most real estate dealers believe that the continuing long-range trend will be upward.

Rising Prices

A widely read magazine for the home building industry has reported that average land prices have more than tripled in the last decade and some suburban property has increased as much as 2,000 per cent.

Less than a year ago some friends of mine looked at a piece of land and were quoted a price of $100,000. They countered with an $85,000 offer. The owner sold to another party for his asking price. The new owners resold to a third party for $135,000 and recently my friends bought the same land for $165,000–all in less than 12 months.

Three years ago I optioned 30 acres of land for $1,500 an acre for a government housing project. The land was rejected and I secured an acceptable tract. The rejected land was then purchased by another party, developed as an industrial park, and sold at an average price of more than $15,000 an acre.

Atlanta newspapers report recent annual price increases in land in that area of 20 per cent. A columnist writing for the *Miami Herald* reported a 46 per cent increase in the cost of single family dwellings in Palm Beach County, Florida in 1972–a sizable portion of this could be attributed to increased land costs.

Farmland

Information supplied by agricultural economics departments of leading land-grant universities reflect pressures on farmland prices from non-farmers–many from out of state who are purchasing land as an inflation hedge and for hideaways, retreats, second homes or for a place to retire away from the noise, smog, traffic and high taxes.

The Economic Research Service of the United States Department of Agriculture reported that average farm real estate prices advanced 75 per cent during the 1960's and average prices advanced 10 per cent in one year–1972. In some states the average price increase for 1972 was more than 20 per cent.

These are average prices. Undoubtedly the rise in value in many selected parcels has been several times this great.

More than 27 million farm acres were bought and sold from March 1971 to March 1972 as compared to 19 million acres one year previous.

Home Sites—Industrial Property

The average cost of a site for a home where a HUD insured mortgage was used doubled in the 1960's with the median size of lots used dropping about 20 per cent in the same period.

A survey of residential and industrial realtors across the country indicates a 200 per cent to 400 per cent increase in raw land since 1950.

Second Homes

Vacation, weekend and second home lots are booming. The American Land Development Association, a trade organization, says there are now 9,000 vacation land development firms in the country. Their sales account for 600 to 700 thousand lots annually for a total price in excess of one-half billion dollars. The average price for a one-quarter acre site is about $7,300.

Competition from Large Corporations

Large corporations are competing for a slice of the pie. Chrysler Realty Company, owned by the Chrysler Corporation, has invested a half billion dollars in real estate and expects this figure to double by 1980.

Westinghouse has a giant land development near Fort Lauderdale, Florida and is starting another mammoth project near Naples.

Ford Motor Company has invested heavily in improved real estate and industrial sites in Michigan.

The list goes on and on and undoubtedly the real estate activity of giant corporations in the real estate market is one other factor behind the rapidly increasing prices.

Multifamily Housing

The trend toward multifamily housing has made fortunes for many who acquired or optioned agricultural or low density land

and got it zoned to a higher density. Price increases of $5,000 an acre or more are not unusual without adding any improvements—just changing the zoning.

Foreign Lands Advancing

The United States had no monopoly on the boom. Houses and lots in Britain have been rising 20 per cent to 40 per cent a year since 1970; Japan has been experiencing a 20 per cent annual increase in land prices. In Canada urban land prices have increased nearly 100 per cent in the last decade and in West Germany, where a tax is being proposed on the rise in land values, some small firms are selling factory sites to building speculators.

It has been quite a while since Will Rogers said, "buy land, they're not making any more of it,"—but perhaps the message is just now getting through.

My challenge, however, does not stop with making you aware of the real estate boom. I want to point out to you how to take advantage of booms when they occur—how to make money in less favorable markets—and how to survive the recessions.

Holding Land Can Be Expensive

Advancing right along with land prices has been the cost of holding land. Some people have the misconception they have made a profit anytime they sell property for more than the purchase price, particularly when they have paid cash. This is far from true. The interest foregone in a cash investment would be at least 5 per cent per annum on today's market. Interest paid on a land mortgage will likely be 8 per cent or more—then you must add real estate taxes, liability insurance and compensation for your time.

Conservatively, the cost of holding a piece of land will amount to 9 or 10 per cent a year under today's conditions. Some studies show that the price of a piece of speculative land must double every seven years to justify holding it. I recommend that if you do not believe the price will double in three to four years—don't buy it.

My purpose is not to show you how to buy average land at average prices, but how to buy a bargain–hold for a short period–and sell for a profit.

2

LAND AND PEOPLE

While every year, with our increasing population, there is less land for each individual—we face no real danger of a land shortage in our time.

Counting acreage of all sorts, mainland United States still has nearly ten acres per capita with about three acres per capita being highly arable (suitable for cultivation). This compares with a little more than an acre of arable land per capita for the world as a whole.

Land Being Absorbed

From 1945 to 1954 the acreage of land in urban areas, highways, airports and reservoirs increased an average of 831,000 acres a year. This is equivalent to 2,441 acres per day.

The above listed purposes were not all of those for which rural land was used. According to the 1963 Yearbook of Agriculture the average rate of absorption of rural land during the 1950's was about 2 million acres per year—or 5,480 acres per day. Some estimates indicate that this figure has doubled in the 1970's.

The chief reason why this vast amount of agricultural land being removed from production each year causes no great alarm is the ever increasing efficiency of the American farmer.

Population Densities and the Future

While three acres per capita seems a reassuring statistic in comparing us with our neighbors of the world, a little more than a hundred years ago the figure was 20 acres per capita. Based on present population forecasts we will be close to the present world average of one and one-fourth acres of arable land per capita by the year 2000.

Total land in the contiguous mainland is 1,904 million acres and about 15 per cent of all the cultivated land in the world lies between our borders. With today's population of approximately 210 million we have density of close to 70 persons per square mile as compared to more than 500 persons per square mile in the densely populated countries such as Japan and Holland and three to ten persons per square mile in sparsely populated areas such as Canada and Australia.

MAJOR CATEGORIES OF OWNERSHIP OF MAINLAND U.S.

	Million Acres	Per cent of Total
Owned by the federal government	408	21
Managed by the federal government, for the Indians	57	3
Owned by the states	80	4
Owned by the counties and municipalities	17	1
Remainder—presumably owned privately, including corporations, co-operatives, trusts, etc.	1,342	71
Total	1,904	100

Declining Birthrate

According to the Census Bureau the nation's birthrate, for the first time ever, dropped to a level during 1972 that could lead to zero population. The fertility rate during this period was about 2.1 births per woman. This is the so-called replacement level—the rate at which the population, in the absence of immigration, would replace itself, and in 70 years reach zero growth—where births equal deaths.

From a speculator's viewpoint we are not particularly concerned with the very long range but a projection of future population, based on birthrates of the last 20 years, is startling.

At the rate of population increase, which has prevailed since 1950, there would be nearly two billion people living in the United States in the year 2100—or about one person per acre of total land surface—mountains, deserts and all. By about 2500 or 2600 the number would reach 3,000 billion—or one person per square yard.

The obvious conclusion is that our birthrate of recent years must be reduced—and most recent figures indicate that we are now beginning a birthrate which will level off the population long before a crisis is at hand—else the trends growing out of our own culture, greater fertility and greater longevity, would be the seeds of our own destruction.

Shifting Uses—More Difficult

Large shifts in major land use will be less common in the next few decades; however, urban areas will continue to absorb farmlands. As land improvements are upgraded, changes are made with more difficulty and at greater costs. The intensity of present uses will doubtless increase—with fewer farm acres feeding more people and fewer residential acres housing larger numbers of our population.

POPULATION TRENDS

In view of the fact that there appears to be enough land, our chief concern is not in how much there is—but where it is and who wants to buy it.

Your aim will be to buy property for resale where people want to work and live—while also keeping in mind second home and recreational demands.

Real estate sales have been brisk in metropolitan suburbs in recent years as a result of people leaving the central cities. Our mobile society accounts for much of our real estate business. Nearly 40 million Americans, or one in five, change homes each year and 13 million of these people migrate across county lines.

Your opportunities will be greater for real estate speculation if you reside in one of the major growth areas. Many fortunes, however, have been made by real estate traders in communities which were losing population. Also, if you live in a small community, don't overlook the possibilities of selling farm and forest lands to city residents hundreds of miles away.

At the turn of the century 60 per cent of our population was rural. In 1970 about 70 per cent of our people lived in metropolitan areas. Urban dwellers are expected to account for 85 per cent of our population by the year 2000.

Rural Population Small—Farm Prices Good

Today, farmers, farm workers and their families are only about 5 per cent of the nation's population. With so few people farming, one might expect prices of farmland to be depressed. The opposite is true. Near the cities—farmland is being gobbled up for subdivisions. More and more affluent city people are buying farms as a hedge against inflation, depreciation for income tax advantages, and for second homes.

In many areas, farms are commanding such high prices that farmers cannot afford to buy them. In most areas your best prospects for farms are professional people living in cities with doctors heading the list. I know some small towns where every doctor is a farm owner. Perhaps it is the need to get away and relax, or the tax advantages a farm can offer, but for whatever reasons, there are places where doctors would rather be "without a stethoscope" than deprived of a good piece of farmland.

Demand for farm property for recreational purposes will continue to grow. More and more people will be using golf courses, fishing lakes, camping sites and just getting away to the outdoors.

By the year 2000 incomes will nearly double and hours of leisure will rise.

Where One Broker Found a Market

A few years ago I became acquainted with a lady real estate broker in a small remote county seat town in West Virginia. She was an astute, successful business woman and was specializing in farm property.

With the extremely low per capita income in this and surrounding communities, I could not imagine how she could sell so much property. She revealed to me that she regularly advertised in Washington, D.C. newspapers and a large percentage of her sales were made to customers in that city and other metropolitan areas in which Washington papers circulate.

"Why would these people buy farms in a strange community so far away," I asked.

She explained that they want to get away from the maddening pace, congestion, bumper to bumper traffic, crime in the streets, and many planned to use their farms for weekends and vacations for a few years–then as a permanent home when they retired.

"I sold a farm to one man who has already moved his family here and drives back and forth to Washington, D.C. every weekend," she said.

Where People Want to Live

A survey conducted by the Opinion Research Corporation in 1971, and included in the report made by the commission on Population Growth and the American Future, offers the following interesting results:

	WHERE DO YOU LIVE NOW? (PER CENT)	WHERE WOULD YOU PREFER TO LIVE? (PER CENT)
Open Country	12	34
Small Town or City	33	30
Medium-sized City or Suburb	28	22
Larger City or Suburb	27	14
	100	100

Another recent survey indicated a preference for living in smaller places—but within commuting distance of a large city.

Change in Growth Regions

While the great population growth is in the metropolitan areas, the growth regions have changed drastically.

A high degree of metropolitan concentration was first developed by the industrial areas of the north. Two-thirds of the northeast was urban by 1900.

Recently, however, the most rapid growth has been in the South, and West and the North seems to be losing much of its magnetism.

In 1900 more than 80 per cent of the South was rural—now more than half is metropolitan. The Atlanta area grew by 37 per cent during the 1960's. The Texas metropolitan population increased by 24 per cent from 1960 to 1970 and in the West, Arizona's population grew 42 per cent from 1960 to 1970.

California has been one of the hot growth areas of recent decades—mostly from migration. More than 90 per cent of California's population lives in metropolitan areas. Annual migration to this state has subsided but population continues to increase as a result of so many young adults who arrived there and are now raising families.

3

GETTING STARTED

Successful real estate trading doesn't necessarily go hand in hand with brilliant minds or college degrees. More power to you if you possess both, but a desire to learn, a positive mental attitude, and a willingness to work and make sacrifices are the keys to getting started. If you can answer the following questions affirmatively you have taken the first step.

1. *Do you anticipate a continuing expanding economy accompanied by inflation?* There are a few businesses which tend to flourish during recessions or major depressions–but real estate speculation is not among them. True, there have been a few fortunes made by individuals who had cash and bought distress property during recessions or depressions. Discount this approach because the chances of your having large sums of cash, should a depression recur, are remote and forecasting accurately, if and when such an economic condition will appear, is impossible.
2. *Can you save a nest egg?* If you have not trained yourself to save a part of your earnings you are not a good candidate for successful real estate speculation or any other business endeavor. Approximately three out of ten families spend more each year than they earn. If you are the head of such a household you are not ready for this business. If you have a proven ability to save but panic at the thought of drawing money out of a bank or savings and loan association, your rewards may not offset your misery.

You must save some money and believe you can reap a greater return, through real estate investment, than lending it to a bank or savings and loan.

3. *Do you believe in yourself?* A fear of losing your job, losing your health, or going broke is normal to the human race, but must be controlled. Most of the things we worry about never happen. Look around you and see numbers of people who have made a financial success, most of them without any recognizable traits of brilliance, but ordinary individuals who had the ambition to try and the will to persist. Fearing your inability to succeed will cause worry and anxiety which destroys your efficiency and paralyzes your ability.
4. *Are you enthusiastic about real estate?*
5. *Will you learn all you can about the real estate business?* Actually, fear and lack of confidence are often caused by lack of knowledge.

WHERE TO START–THINGS TO KNOW

The beginning speculator should start in familiar surroundings–his own town or county. This point cannot be overemphasized. Don't go chasing deals in another state or across the country until you learn the fundamentals at home.

Your own town, county, or borough is the best place to start. Naturally, your opportunities will be more limited if you live in a very small community. There are always, however, some residential and commercial possibilities and sometimes vast opportunities in surrounding farmlands.

Bruce Barton once wrote the following: "The other day I visited the suburb where I used to live. There was a vacant lot opposite my house which could have been bought then for five thousand dollars. A month ago a man bought it for twenty eight thousand, and two weeks later sold it for sixty thousand. I take off my hat to him. He saw it as a gold mine. But I looked at it every morning for four years, and it didn't look to me like anything more than a vacant lot."

Once you get the feel of selecting, buying, and selling–then you may want to look into opportunities in a nearby city or town. Just be sure to confine your beginning efforts to an area with which you can become entirely familiar—not more than a short drive away. Don't ever put yourself in competition with those who know better than you the area, the demand, the growth potential, and all the factors which influence prices.

Brokers Can Be Helpful

Although most of my transactions are not made through brokers, I have always found it wise to become personally acquainted with one or two good brokers in my community. Quite often these people may help you make a good purchase or sale—then if you use their services from time to time, you can go to them for advice on properties which they are not listing.

My preference is a young, hustling firm—or if you use an older established firm, a young aggressive salesman in their firm will usually be your best bet. Older firm members often concentrate their efforts on established clients—larger deals—and many spend a lot of their time in property management.

Undeveloped Property

Your best bet is to begin with raw (undeveloped) property. Buy property which, through your efforts or natural growth patterns, will elevate to a *higher* use.

Agricultural land, which has potential residential use, residential land zoned for single family housing which can be rezoned for multifamily housing, or any residentially classified land which in the forseeable future has commercial or industrial potentials, is a good bet.

Land which has already reached its highest potential use level is generally a poor investment. Chances are that it will be worth more dollars each succeeding year but this is an inflationary gain rather than a true value gain.

Generally, the advantages of raw land over developed property are lower investment, less taxes, and fewer management problems.

We do not rule out developed property for the beginner, however, and in later chapters will suggest types of properties to consider in order to maximize profits and minimize risks.

Things to Know—Tools to Use

You will need a few basic tools to get start[...] are usually readily available and either free or [...]

1. Obtain the latest and best maps of your [...] scale, the better. These are usually avai[...] your city chamber of commerce, local industr[...] commission or your local or state highway departments.
2. Supplement the above with any zoning maps available from the proper local governmental agency—usually a city or metropolitan planning commission.
3. Secure a copy of your local zoning regulations. These should give you density restrictions, height restrictions, set-back requirements, parking requirements, and other information which restrict land use.
4. Make use of topographic maps when available. These can be obtained in many areas through local dealers or may be ordered directly from your state geologist. The scale is small—one inch = 2,000 feet—and vertical contours are at 20 feet intervals. Yet they show buildings, power lines, rivers, lakes, and so forth and identify the wooded areas. This mapping program is still in process and is incomplete. I have been fortunate, however, in finding those available in most areas where I have developed real estate.

   Most large communities have one or more photo-copy facilities which can enlarge these to a more readable scale—say one inch = 200 feet. Architects and land planners use their enlarged maps as an inexpensive method of preparing preliminary site lay-outs. Since some error results from this much enlargement, new topo maps established by ground survey crews or aerial photography may be needed for final plans.
5. Become familiar with all applicable property taxes. This is extremely important—particularly if you hold a parcel of property for an extended period—since this becomes one of your major expense items.

   Property taxes vary so greatly from area to area that examples of a specific area or even national average would be of little use to you. Become familiar with how taxes are your area. What individual or agency does the ...? What is the relationship between true or market ...e and assessed value? This can vary from locality to locality from as little as 10 per cent to as much as 100 per cent.

The annual taxes are computed by multiplying the assessed value by your tax rate. Example follows:

A one acre commercial lot has a true value of $40,000. For tax purposes 50 per cent of the true value is used resulting in an assessed value for tax purposes of $20,000. The tax rate is $4 per $100. Annual taxes would be $800 per year.

Find out the due date for taxes. The tax year may be the same as the calendar year, or may relate to a fiscal year–July through June, or any other arbitrary 12 months fiscal period established by the local government.

Some governments offer a small discount for early payment; others only establish a date beyond which taxes are delinquent and a penalty is assessed.

Become familiar with each agency having taxing authority. There may be only one–there could be three or more. When more than one agency collects taxes, the rates, valuations, and due dates may be the same or entirely different.

6. Review local annexation laws. In some instances cities or municipal governments may arbitrarily extend their boundaries. In other areas this requires the consent of the majority of the citizens in the area proposed for annexation. Either of these procedures or variations may apply to your area. Obtain the correct information from your local governing agency.

   The possibility of annexation may enhance or detract from the value of property which you are about to buy or sell. The property should be worth more if increased services–better schools, water, sewer, fire protection, better streets, and so forth–are immediately available.

   Often many of these services are not immediately available and may be many years off. Yet, new taxes are imposed as soon as property is annexed. This can deflate the value of property.

7. Learn all you can about local, available financing. Generally speaking, your sources will be: (a) commercial banks; (b) savings and loan associations; (c) mortgage companies; (d) individuals.

   Look to commercial banks only for short-term capital. Some will loan for 16 years or longer but generally prefer much shorter loans—ninety days, six months, one year, and so forth.

   The charter of some commercial banks precludes them from loaning on unimproved property, i.e., vacant land.

   Savings and loan associations do permanent financing, i.e., long-term mortgages.

   Mortgage companies lend for insurance companies, savings and loan associations, and commercial banks.

   Individuals from whom you buy property will often accept a nominal down payment and carry the balance over a period of years. There may be other individuals in your community who lend on real estate mortgages at about the same rate or for a little more than charged by banks or savings and loan associations. A more complete description of available money is given in the chapter on "Financing."

8. Attempt to attend every real estate auction in your area. There is no better way to stay current on property values. Your ability to capitalize on this source will depend on where you live. The auction method of selling real estate is extremely popular in some areas and virtually nonexistent in others. Real estate auctions are discussed fully in another chapter.

9. Explore your area and look for brokers' signs on property. If you spot a tract in which you are interested and it has no sign—stop and inquire. You will pass up many good buys if you take a negative attitude—"I know he wouldn't sell." Quite often you will be surprised, and even if the owner of a particular piece of property is not interested, he may suggest another party who has a similar piece of property who is interested in selling.

10. Rely upon classified newspaper advertisements as an excellent source of information. Read these regularly and particularly those in your Sunday edition. If any of the properties described interest you, but you are not in a position to buy, clip these and file for future use.
11. If you contemplate trading in farmland, acquaint yourself with your county agricultural agent and the director of your local Soil Conservation Service.

    These people are not real estate appraisers, but generally speaking they will know the value of the property *today* for the purpose for which it is being used. They may also give you some good leads on who is interested in selling. Your challenge is to estimate what the value will be at a later date–perhaps based on a higher use. The Soil Conservation Service has aerial photos of all the property in your county. You can study these free of charge or buy them for a very nominal price. Allow a few weeks for delivery. A special viewing device in most soil conservation offices will give you a three-dimensional picture.

Learn the Fundamentals

Admittedly, most of the foregoing are rather elementary. Nevertheless, they are important if you are interested in becoming a serious amateur in this business.

This book is written for those of you who need to generate additional income. Doing your homework and using a systematic approach will pay off. My specific suggestions will be brief and limited. If we make real estate trading sound boring, rather than fun, we have already defeated our purpose. The most that I hope to do is to give you a few sound fundamentals on which to build.

Many golfers play all their lives without ever taking a lesson. Most will admit that they regret not taking a few lessons in the beginning–enough to build a sound swing. This would have taken none of the fun out of the game–to the contrary, it would have made the game more enjoyable and reduced their scores.

For some strange reason, many people assume that they were born with all the knowledge they need on real estate, but everything has to be learned about the stock market. The publi library in my home town lists 25 books on speculation. Twenty-three of these are on stocks and commodities and only two on real estate—yet, greater numbers of people own real estate.

Perhaps one reason why more has not been written on real estate speculation in recent years may be that it has been so *easy* to trade profitably in real property. The increasing population and growing economy has protected many from bad deals.

I have traded in real estate for 25 years with only one small loser. While I have been lucky, I firmly believe I could have doubled or tripled my earnings if I had taken the trouble to learn more of the fundamentals in the beginning.

SETTING YOUR GOALS

It is important that you conclude in your own mind what you hope to achieve.

Do not aim too low but be realistic. Not only should you be realistic in assessing your ability but also be realistic in determining the sacrifices you are willing to endure to reach certain pinnacles.

I have seen some men gain enormous wealth at the expense of neglecting their families or wrecking their health—only to be miserable when they had achieved what they thought they wanted.

The amount of speculation in which you can engage will depend upon available capital, available time, and your enthusiasm for the undertaking.

Obviously, if you deal in improved property requiring repairs, maintenance, and management, this will be more time consuming than buying and selling vacant land or raw property.

Goals often change with age. Advancing years are no great handicap in this business. As a matter of fact, I have seen many active speculators up in their 80's. It does, however, have a bearing on the type of property purchased and on how it is purchased. Generally speaking, older persons are attracted to property which required little maintenance and management.

They most often buy for cash or amortize over a short period of time and sell in the same manner. Through this approach they lose some leveraging advantages, but shrewdness, gained through years of experience, is an offsetting factor, and having more cash than their younger competitors will enable them to make some excellent purchases.

Except in very rare situations, I confine my speculation efforts to vacant land. I find it requires three to four years to turn the property over at a good profit—some much quicker, and some longer—but this is average. I am never happy with an annual return on my investment of less than 20 per cent to 25 per cent. I try to buy land in a transitional stage, located where it is likely to be in greater demand for the purpose for which it is now used, or preferably a higher use in three to five years.

Factors Influencing Value

Four things which can usually be relied upon to increase the price of your property are:

1. Inflation.
2. Growth and transition of area where located.
3. The improvements which you make to the property.
4. Subdivision of your property.

The first two are beyond your control. You are only betting they happen. The third and fourth, however, are in your hands.

With regard to number three, I find that a farm tool called a *bush-hog,* which is a large rotary mower operating from a tractor power take-off, is excellent and economical for cleaning up land. If you trade extensively in large tracts, you may want to own one, but you may be able to contract for these by the hour. Depending on where you live and the size of the tractor and the mower, the price range for the tractor, rotary mower, and operator will cost from $6 to $15 an hour. As a rule, the mower will cut anything that can be pushed over with the tractor. Extremely large growth will require a bulldozer.

On large tracts after bush-hogging, go over the ground with a harrow, fertilize and lime liberally, and sow in grass. Use a bulldozer for filling gullies, cutting roads, and for piling and burning rubbish. Do not attempt to change contours or grades on large tracts. This becomes very expensive; leave it to the developer.

If you are dealing with an expensive commercial lot, it may pay you to spend several hundred or even thousands of dollars to grade to street level.

If improving a timber tract you may want to leave all the trees and bush-hog the undergrowth making the land more attractive and easier to show to your prospect. I have seen the owners of many pieces of raw land double their money in a few months after cleaning them up and sowing in grass.

Subdividing will require more time and money but certainly may be worth considering. This is treated in detail in another section of this book.

If you desire some property income each year and your average turnover is three or four years, you should strive to inventory four or more parcels. You cannot establish a month and day on which you will sell a given parcel of land, but you need to plan your work, then work your plan as in any other undertaking.

Your most important venture may be your first one. Nothing which you read or no one with whom you advise, will be an adequate substitute for investing your own money, getting the property ready for sale, finding a buyer, and cashing out for a profit. Once you have done this you will be on your way. It may take you five years to save up for your first purchase but once you get the speculation fever, which usually comes with a profitable trade, you may be hooked for life.

Reiterating a note of caution–liquidity, or the lack of it, can be a problem at times. Do not be afraid or too cautious, but do not become reckless and overextend. You may be within six or twelve months of doubling your money but have to sell out at a break-even or loss if you become pressed for capital.

Various theories have been advanced as to how much capital a real estate speculator should keep in reserve. Some say 25 per cent of your working capital–some say more–some less. I believe each individual must work this out with common sense.

USE YOUR OWN JUDGMENT

A friend of mine has been in and out of real estate all of his life but never made any real money in the process.

A personable sort of fellow who has many contacts, he seems to forever be running into good buys but through lack of confidence in his own judgment, he seldom converts them to profit.

When he finds something *hot* he immediately gathers up some friends and drives them by the property to get his opinion confirmed. One of two things happens:

1. One or more of his consultants find fault with the deal and he cools off, or;
2. In many instances some of his friends to whom he shows the property, buy it while he is making up his mind.

An Expensive Lesson

Several years ago I moved to a new community and since I had recently disposed of some property, started looking around for an investment.

I found a strip of highway property which attracted my attention and being a stranger to the community I went to a real estate agent to inquire about it. The agent immediately started pointing out the bad points of the property and talking to me about a *much better buy* which he had listed.

I permitted myself to be *touted* off this property, although I did learn from the agent that it belonged to an out of town owner who wouldn't sell. Three months later, three individuals bought the property from the out-of-towner who wouldn't sell for $33,000, subdivided it, and sold it at auction in less than one year for $112,000.

My first mistake was in not contacting the owner regarding his interest in selling. The second mistake was in seeking and taking advice prejudiced by the agent's own selfish interest. Never rely on advice on any matter from a biased source or from someone who does not know more than you about the subject.

As in any other business, confidence will come with experience. So many judgment factors must be applied that the novice often becomes confused and sometimes downright frightened. A few good trades under his belt will usually cure this. If it doesn't, he should forget all about it.

Never Look Back

One of the greatest problems is looking back. The chances are that if you are looking at a $20,000 commercial lot, half of the people to whom you reveal your interest in the property can remember when it sold for $1,500, and some of *these* will judge its present day's value by a sale years ago.

A few years ago I bought a piece of commercial property for $12,000. The neighbors delighted in letting me know that three years prior it had sold for delinquent taxes—a fact which I, of course, found out during the title search. Sometime thereafter I sold the property for $20,500 and the new owner undoubtedly was again reminded of how he could have acquired it for nothing a few years back.

If you are considering buying property, the price which the present owner paid should be the least of your concern. This can only have any meaning at all if his acquisition was recent and representative of prices for the same kind of property in the same neighborhood.

Concern yourself with zoning, utilities, subdividing, converting to a higher use, and so forth. Let the neighbors worry about the fact that it was much cheaper a few years back. Good opportunities are missed every day by persons who lose their courage after talking with pessimistic neighbors and friends. Apparently this has been going on for a long time as we see from the following interesting story by Benjamin Franklin:

> There are croakers in every country, always boding its ruin. Such a one lived in Philadelphia; a person of note, an elderly man with a wise look and a very grave manner of speaking; his name was Samuel Mickle. This gentleman, a stranger to me, stopped one day at my door and asked me if I was the young man who had lately opened a new printing house. Being answered in the affirmative, he said he was sorry for me, because it was an expensive undertaking, and the expense would be lost; for Philadelphia was a sinking place, the people already half bankrupt or near being so; all appearances to the contrary, such as new buildings and rise of rents, being to his certain knowledge fallacious, for they were, in fact, among the things that would soon ruin us. And he

gave me such a detail of misfortunes now existing, or that were soon to exist, that he left me half melancholy. Had I known this before I engaged in business, probably I never should have done it. This man continued to live in this decaying place, and to disclaim in the same strain, refusing for many years to buy a house there, because all was going to destruction, and at last I had the pleasure of seeing him give five times as much for one as he might have bought it for when he first began croaking.

Advice to Take—and Not to Take

Normally the three people with whom you must acquaint your decision to purchase (or sell) are—your banker, your lawyer, and your accountant.

Three people with whom you should *not* rely on as to *value* are—your banker, your lawyer, and your accountant.

A speculator expects a greater than normal profit from taking a greater than normal risk—bankers do not think like this—nor should they.

Since any generalization is unfair, I am happy to agree that there are exceptions to people in the above professions not being sources of sound advice on real estate values. The exceptions usually occur when these people themselves are speculators or investors. All of them have, of course, witnessed more transactions than you—but I don't count this. Speculation is not a spectator sport. Unless an individual has had his own money riding on a deal—won some and lost some—but won more, you should not rely too heavily on his judgment.

By the same token these people can be invaluable to you with the "mechanics" of the deal. Some trades that look good to you may be bad after your accountant analyzes how it affects your taxes. Take his advice on these matters. Certainly a good attorney can steer you away from a lot of legal pitfalls and if you don't have credit established with your banker, you probably can't speculate—period!

Greatest Problem

The greatest single problem of the real estate trader is that of maintaining a sufficiently liquid position to permit taking advantage of good deals when they arise. This can sometimes be solved by joint venturing with a financial partner. The problem is greater for the raw property speculator than for those who deal in improved property and can rely to some degree on the cash flow generated by rents.

4

REAL ESTATE VERSUS COMMON STOCKS

In all likelihood, you have already made your choice as to the work you will pursue to support your family. Whether you are an employee, own a business, or engage in a profession—the chances are you regularly save a portion of your income.

You have likely concluded you cannot afford to keep all of your surplus earnings in cash, a savings account, or government bonds. Many who have made this obvious conclusion are still not doing anything about it because of lack of time, energy, or courage. It has been said that most people are too busy making a living to make any money.

Aside from emergency funds or the necessity for liquid assets for ear-marked purposes, surplus capital should be used to buy something which has a *growth potential* in order to avoid the erosion of inflation.

Government bonds, the five year—ten month maturity type, bought by most individuals, yield 5 per cent compounded semi-annually when held to maturity.

Savings accounts, other than long term certificates, pay 4 to 6 per cent, hardly offsetting losses from inflation. Living costs have increased by leaps and bounds, and costs of sending a youngster through college have skyrocketed. A house which you could have bought for $20,000 in 1960 will cost you $40,000 today, and the price of a ten day stay in the hospital has more than doubled since 1960.

Obviously then, your surplus funds must be tied to the growth of the economy and the inflation of the dollar.

Some of you will have concluded that at best your potential earnings from your present job offers little hope of more than a living income and may be flirting with the idea of starting your own small business. Americans down through the years have taken this route to greater financial rewards—millions successfully. Outnumbering those who succeeded, however, are the combination of those whose financial rewards were no better than could have been anticipated as an employee of a large firm, and those who didn't make it at all.

I believe that many can achieve their desired earnings level, while maintaining the security of full-time employment, by using their spare time and capital for real estate speculation.

While there are many commodities on which you can bet today's cost against tomorrow's selling price, including antiques, rare coins, and dozens of others, the average individual who invests or speculates will make his choice between real estate and common stocks.

More than 30 million persons own common stocks, and many more than this own real estate when you take into consideration home owners.

The pure investor—the individual who is looking for income and/or possibly creating an estate for his children or grandchildren—may find good stocks or good real estate about equally rewarding. Based on the past and using long range figures, the investor who has bought and held Eastman Kodak or a well located commercial building or an apartment complex has done well. The annual income will likely have been greater on the real estate, but the growth or appreciation greater on the stock.

In receiving a greater annual return, the real estate investor will likely have also spent more time in management, and too he would have had a far less liquid asset. On the other hand, he may have been able to use his depreciation to shelter other income.

Now, we move away from *investment* to *speculation* and make some comparisons. Real estate offers several important advantages:

1. More leverage. Less equity cash is required and property can often be paid for over a period of time.

2. Less risky. On the average, the market value on a parcel of real estate fluctuates less and is not nearly so sensitive to local, national, and world conditions or rumors in the wind.
3. Greater knowledge of your holdings. This enables you to exercise more intelligent control.
4. Less commission expenses. In many instances you can avoid paying any commissions by selling your own property. If you use a broker you will only pay commission when you sell. If you trade in stocks, you pay a commission when you purchase and again when you sell.

Whereas some real estate purchases require all cash, and many transactions specify 29 per cent down, by persistent searching you can find good investments on favorable terms. Often purchases can be made with no more than 10 per cent down and as long as five or ten years to pay the balance at going bank rate interest or less.

While the price of any commodity not artifically supported or controlled by the government is in the final analysis based on the law of supply and demand, individual issues of stock are caught up in market trends. It is common to see the price of a given stock rise during a period when earnings are dropping off and even with management weakening. Conversely, the stock may fall during periods of stronger earnings, better management, and prospects for improved business.

Real estate with minor exceptions is bought and sold at prices bearing a close relationship to the value of the land to a potential user.

I once bought a stock listed on the New York Stock Exchange–watched the price climb to above 90–split two for one–sold in the 40's range for a few weeks–started down–and in less than a year was at five. It is highly questionable whether the stock was ever worth 90 dollars, but there were no rational reasons reflected in the operating or balance sheet for this behavior. This kind of fluctuation is unheard of in real estate, with the possible exception of a few isolated booms created by fast-buck promoters–such as the Florida boom of the 1920's.

Andrew Carnegie, one of the early financial giants of our country, was a strong believer in real estate and had this to say about the subject: "Ninety per cent of all millionaires become so through owning real estate. More money has been made in real estate than in all industrial investments combined. The wise young man or wage earner invests his money in real estate."

Stock market traders are easily stampeded and frequently behave like sheep. The least ripple changes them from optimists to pessimists or vice versa, and they follow the leader—even though no one knows who the leader is—to buy or sell. In contrast, while overall economic conditions affect the real estate market, there is no rush to buy or sell based on isolated happenings or rumors, and sales of land may be brisk and prices high in Houston while trading has slacked off and prices are down in St. Paul.

While there is an abundance of written information available on all listed companies, in contrast to none on most real estate, it is often of little or no use. Forecasters, like race track touts, get lucky occasionally, but studies in the past have revealed that random selections—such as throwing darts at *Wall Street Journal*—would have resulted in better selections. Reputable brokerage houses and analysts can give you an abundance of facts, but they have not proven to be exceptionally clarivoyant as to when to buy, when to sell, what to pay, and how much to sell.

The absence of widely disseminated information and forecasts on real estate prices may be a blessing in disguise. You will have to use your own judgment, and for this reason you will become better informed.

Despite all the controls, there is still a lot of *hanky panky* on the part of insiders of some large listed companies. My experience as a real estate consultant for a subsidiary of a large conglomerate led me to believe that greater emphasis was given to making a favorable impression on the stock analyst than was placed on sound business principles which would ultimately bring real profits to the investors. Accounting procedures seemed designed more to reflect favorable quarterly statements than to give a true picture to the shareholders.

Many stock brokerage firms have not presented the image of a safe harbor for the security minded. Hopefully, the 1968-70 chaotic period in which scores of brokerage firms vanished, taking along sizable sums of their client's savings, has caused the institution of new regulations for protecting clients.

Traditionally, brokers have used their client's stocks as bank collateral in borrowing funds to finance their margin customers and often for their own investing.

Often information which you need for making decisions on stocks is not available to you until long after the insiders have capitalized on it and it is too late to salvage your position.

Complicated bookkeeping systems, whether or not actually designed to deceive you, can make it next to impossible to decipher a corporate operating statement.

Much of the fun, challenge, and excitement is lost when you trade in stocks because you have passed along the responsibilities to others. In real estate, you are the coach of the team—sending in plays and making substitutions. In stocks, you are betting on the game through the corner bookie. The game plan and even the odds are devised by other persons for you.

There are, however, no perfect type investments and if you trade in real estate, keep in mind the following drawbacks:

1. Lack of liquidity.
2. Shortage of reliable statistical data.
3. Uncertainty of local taxes.
4. Management problems with developed property.
5. Time consumption of real estate trading.

You can buy and sell common stocks over the telephone, through a broker who will, if you desire, advise you when to buy and when to sell.

If you need to turn your stocks to cash in a hurry, you can phone your broker from anywhere in the world and your money is available in three days. Converting real estate into cash usually takes much longer.

Regardless of what is written or even proven, millions of individuals will continue to speculate in stocks *and* real estate. Some see the stock market as part of the foundation of this country—a place where you buy shares in America. Others see it as a big poker game. Perhaps it is some of both.

Regardless of where you speculate, there is only one real determining factor of the price you will receive—that is what another person will be willing to pay you for what you have to sell.

Your object is to buy cheap and sell high, but this is also the object of all your competitors; so, be sure you play the game *well*.

If you are already hooked on either of these games, presumably you will be influenced by the results which you are getting. If you are just now ready to begin putting your surplus capital to work, may I make a suggestion which will likely have more influence on your decision than a volume of statistical information. Consult with five or ten mature, successful business men in your community who have experience both in stock trading and real estate speculation. Find out which endeavor has offered the least risks and returned the greatest rewards.

5

RAW LAND AND PROFITS

The greatest opportunities for speculators with limited time and capital are in raw (unimproved) land. Adam Smith, the economist, said, "The purchase and improvement of uncultivated land is the most profitable employment of the smallest, as well as greatest capitals and the road of all the fortune which can be acquired in that country, America."

The primary purpose of this book is to show you how to make money buying and selling this type property. We cannot, however, neglect discussing improved property because without some knowledge of potential uses the owner of raw land cannot evaluate its worth.

Recently I acquired an interest in two parcels of raw real estate—one a 60 acre industrial tract in the heart of a growing metropolitan area—the other a large rural tract with a mile of highway frontage.

Certainly, the physical characteristics of the properties were considered, but the overriding consideration was future value based on projected use of the properties by potential buyers.

Two Properties Compared

In the case of the industrial tract I could not have intelligently purchased this property without some knowledge of what a manufacturer or warehouse operator could afford to pay per acr once the property is developed. It was also necessary that I have knowledge of the costs of installing required streets, utilities, and so forth since I will likely have the property surveyed, topo mapped, and planned, and will then wholesale it to others who will subdivide it, improve it, and sell it on a lot or acreage basis.

The price per acre for the industrial property was approximately ten times the cost of the residential property, yet I believe each will return about the same profit on dollars invested and time spent.

In the case of the rural property, which I contemplate subdividing into lots and tracts, I would not have made the purchase without the possibility of prospective purchasers financing their dwellings through the Farmers Home Administration. The area is not served by a Department of Housing and Urban Development (HUD) approved mortgagee, and I question whether commercial banks and savings and loan associations located some distance away will advance credit in sufficient amounts and at rates conducive to stimulate development.

In every instance you need to know what the buyer can afford to pay in order to profitably develop the land into his intended use. If the land, either because of demand or zoning restrictions, is suitable only for single family residences, and a developer can realize only three lots per acre he may be able to pay you only $3,000 an acre for the raw land. If, however, zoning permits a density of 20 units per acre and there is a demand for rental apartments or condominiums the land may be worth ten or twenty thousand per acre—or more.

Statistics Scarce

Meaningful statistics on real estate are scarce. Long-range price trends on certain types of property particularly farmlands are available but they are based on averages and have little value to the individual who expects to hold the property for a short time and make a much greater than average profit. Your best information will come from a survey of your own surroundings. What about the lots and tracts on the edge of town which were sold this year? How much did they bring? What could you have bought this for three years ago? Six years ago? Ten years ago?

How Much Profit Should You Expect?

Assuming the continuation of the present rising price trend which started with the beginning of recovery from the depression of the 1930's, most of your real estate trades should be winners.

You may have a few losers and make a few killings. Keep in mind, however, the total amount of profit on a winning deal will be in proportion to the amount invested. It is theoretically as easy for the individual investing $100,000 to make $100,000 profit as it is for the man who invests $1,000 to make a $1,000 profit. Actually, it is much easier for the man with $100,000 since large investors have less competition.

You should conservatively expect any vacant property which you are willing to buy to double in price in four years. Some traders have done far better in recent years.

To me a piece of property which with a minimum of improvements does not offer excellent prospects for doubling in price in three to four years or less should be passed up, because there are plenty others on which this return can be anticipated. We are speaking strictly of raw or unimproved property where purchase is made with quick resale in mind–not apartments or commercial buildings for long time investment. Here's how to do it:

1. Buy at 20 per cent below the average market price. "This is great in theory," you say, "but it is ridiculous to believe it can be done." Not so. Even in buying commodities such as automobiles, groceries, and clothes, where prices are somewhat standardized, careful shoppers pay at least 10 per cent less than their careless neighbors.

   On real estate it is easy to do much better than this. No two parcels of real estate are the same. Your knowledge of the future worth of property should be much greater than average, and the price of a piece of real estate is subject to fluctuation based on the circumstances of the owner.

   Automobile factories or retail merchants are not likely to cut prices because sales slow down for a week or a month or a quarter. They are well financed and have heavy investments in plants and stores. While they must adapt to changing economic conditions, price changes come gradually and slowly. Property owners are different. Their attitudes change frequently. They move to new jobs, become ill, age, die, inherit, and have domestic problems. The man who asked $10,000 for a lot a month ago may take $7,500 today because his company is transferring him to another state.

Don't let yourself believe there are no more bargains. There may not be, compared to 1933 prices, but they are everywhere to be found when comparing to other prices being paid today. I have watched shrewd buyers at an auction sale buy lots or tracts at 20 per cent to 30 per cent–even 50 per cent below the average of prices paid by other buyers for similar lots and tracts.

2. Add at least 10 per cent to the value of your property by beautifying it. Get rid of weeds, brush, scrub timber, gullies, and so forth, then fertilize and seed in grass. Not only does this increase its value, it advertises the property. People are curious about changes being made. Working on the property will attract attention. The neighbors will know it changed hands. The knowledge that you had confidence in its future will give others confidence.

   I have seen property lie dormant for years with no apparent interest on the part of buyers, then watch prospects come out of the woodwork when someone buys it and starts changing its appearance.

3. Inflation will add another 20 per cent to the dollar value in three to four years. So by buying a bargain, improving your property, and through inflation, you have added 50 per cent to the value in three or four years.

4. Your big reward should come, however, from growth and expansion of the area. Growth patterns in towns and cities are usually evident and if you bought on the south side of town when the planning commission, the chamber of commerce, or your own careful observation would have told you the growth pattern was west–you goofed.

Exactly how much benefit you will get from this will vary from city to city, area to area, and year to year–but a 50 to 100 per cent increase in three or four years is not unusual.

Drive around your own area and look at the residential subdivisions being built on what was farmland three or four years ago, industrial parks and shopping centers being built on ten thousand or twenty thousand dollars an acre property that could have been bought for a third of this price less than five years ago.

I can prove any of these situations over and over to you on land which I have bought and sold and on transactions of others which I have observed. But, you should gather your own proof from your own area. Look around you for the evidence.

Use Credit to Increase Returns

Even though you sell for twice the amount of your purchase price, if you paid cash, you will not realize a 100 per cent gain because of expenses in buying and selling, beautifying, time expended, and interest foregone on your investment.

Many times, however, these expenses can be offset by leveraging and you can expect a return of 100 per cent or more on your cash invested. Let's consider the following example:

"A" buys a lot for $12,000 and pays cash. His taxes are $200 per year and he spends no money on improvements. He sells at the end of three years for $18,600. He nets $6,000 or 50 per cent on his investment.

"B" buys a lot for $12,000 and pays $3,500 down. He makes no improvements. His principal, interest, and tax payments have amounted to $5,700 at the end of three years–so to date he has an actual cash outlay of $3,600 plus $5,700 or $9,300. He sells his lot for $18,600. He has made a 100 per cent profit on his cash investment since profit is defined as *the excess of returns over expenditures in a transaction or series of transactions.*

Obviously, for tax purposes the cost of the lot plus all expenses would be subtracted from the selling price to obtain profit, and "B" would be taxed on less profit than "A" since his interest is a deductable expense, but he would actually have received a much greater return on his investment of cash. Leveraging makes the difference.

Compensation to Expect

When I sell a piece of property I expect, first of all, a return of all capital outlays and expenses, including cost of property, interest (paid and foregone), taxes, expenditures for improvements, and so forth. In addition, I want to be compensated for the following:

1. Time.
2. Know how.
3. Risk.

Double Your Income

I firmly believe that you can double your present income through knowledgeable and careful real estate speculation—if you are willing to sacrifice to get some surplus capital, work hard, study and learn the business—and take good, calculated risks.

Your first challenge is to raise some surplus capital if you do not already have it. Nothing worthwhile is attained without making some sacrifices. If you are healthy and employed you can save some money.

Many years ago a distant cousin of mine came from the farm where he was reared in a family of modest financial circumstances to Knoxville, Tennessee and got a job as a streetcar conductor. Prior to leaving the farm he became a youthful speculator. He bought and sold chickens, ducks, geese, pigs, and other farm commodities.

From his humble salary as a streetcar conductor he managed to save a little each week. He observed property along his route and discussed various parcels with passengers who lived in the area. When he had a little saved he began buying property. As time went by he not only applied his savings from his salary but used profits from his transactions to make new purchases.

Before retirement age he had become wealthy. He was one of the city's largest property owners and highly respected in the business community for his financial acumen.

Many of today's fortunes were gained by men from humble beginnings. A close friend of mine started in the manufacturing business less than 20 years ago with $500 in capital. Today he owns 50 per cent of the stock in a company doing more than $20 million annual volume.

Another friend, mentioned in the preface, was born in the mountain country of western North Carolina. He never had the opportunity for a formal education. He started working on a farm, got a few dollars ahead, and started trading—first in livestock and later in timber and land. Today his worth is more than a million dollars.

So you see it can be done. The pessimist will lead you to believe that all of the good deals have already been made; the opportunity was yesterday; prices now are too high. Don't be misled; the opportunities are greater than ever. There are more people living on this earth today than all who were born, lived, and died since the beginning of civilization—more people demanding goods and services—lots, homes, farms, warehouses, and commercial buildings.

OPPORTUNITY*

They do me wrong who say I come no more
  When once I knock and fail to find you in,
For every day I stand outside your door
  And bid you wake, and rise to fight and win.

Wail not for precious chances passed away,
  Weep not for golden ages on the wane!
Each night I burn the records of the day;
  At sunrise every soul is born again.

The challenge is up to you. A lot will depend on your self-image. Think of yourself as a winner. Get rid of your negative outlook. Look around you. Pick out the successful people. They had a plan, a goal, and an ambition, and they were willing to sacrifice and work. Talk with them, learn from them, then plan your own program.

If your goal is to double your present income—start saving now. Set your goal at an amount equal to one year's wages but don't wait until you have the entire amount to start speculating. *Use leverage.* Make your first investment when you have enough for your down payment and can amortize the rest over a long enough period to enable you to make payments from what you can expect to save from your salary or wages. Get the most liberal terms possible on the balance. Don't sign a two year note when you can make one for ten. Then if fortune smiles on you, a salary raise or a sale of the property—pay it off ahead of schedule.

*Walter Malone

If you are just beginning:

1. Buy raw property.
2. Be sure you can reasonably expect to make the payments from income other than from the sale of the property.
3. Buy only property which you sincerely believe will double in price within four years or less.

A short while back I sold sixty lots at auction from a tract of raw land which I developed. My profit was satisfactory, but some of the purchasers resold their lots at double their purchase prices, which they paid me, within ten days from the date of the sale.

If your goal is additional income each year and your average time from purchase to sale is three or four years, you will need to inventory three or four parcels so you can expect to sell one each year. To double your present income each year your total investment should be about three times your annual earnings. Actual cash requirement will be less due to leveraging but as you extend your credit your reserves should be greater.

If you believe that doubling your money in three years on a piece of unimproved property is too optimistic, set your goals more conservatively. Maybe you believe it will take five years, or perhaps you want to try to work toward a one or two year turnover but will be satisfied with a 25 per cent or 50 per cent gain. When you reduce the anticipated margin of profit or increase the length of time for turnover, you also increase the capital requirements or need for greater leveraging or both.

To double your spendable income you do not have to actually double the amount of your earnings. Most of your real estate profits will be long term capital gain and taxed at about one-half the rate of your salary or wages.

The Four Year Plan

I suggest you plan your program based on goals of turning your property at double the purchase price every four years. Some properties will be sold in three months after purchase at a good profit. Some may be sold in two years at a 50 per cent gain. The four year plan is suggested after arriving at averages from my own experience. This program is based on continuing demand and rising prices. No one can guarantee these conditions will prevail, but if you do not anticipate them you should not speculate. You could save cash but it will likely be worth much less next year than this year due to erosion of value from inflation.

Even with the long range price trend continuing upward, you may be sure there will be peaks and valleys. These alone should cause you to be careful about overextending and to keep reasonable reserves in fairly liquid assets.

In using the past to mirror the future, we contemplate a clearer image when mirrored in recent years and a hazier one becoming almost unrecognizable, as we look further back. I believe we can perceive more about the eighties by examining the seventies, than we can learn from the sixities.

Probably the most unchanging factor which we are dealing with is human nature itself, and even it seems to have been going through some face lifting in recent years. I have no doubt, however, that future generations, like the past, will cherish land–buy it–sell it–farm it–build on it. Some will improve it, others will exploit it and abuse it. As the population grows there will be fewer acres for each of us.

Those who have specialized in conservative investments with emphasis on income and who have not really examined the potential return on raw property may scoff at the four year plan, but I have discussed this hypothesis with numerous successful speculators who tell me their average turnover, at good profits, is less than four years.

During the last 12 months I have sold five parcels of real estate (other than subdivided lots where profits cannot be accurately calculated until the entire subdivision is sold). The transactions were as follows:

Parcel No. 1 was purchased with approximately $3,000 down with the owner carrying 12 months note for the balance and when I resold it three months later the note was transferred to the new owner–with him picking up the tab for all of the interest on the note. Was my profit of $9,000 a 36 per cent profit? Or was it 300 per cent - since I got $9,000 for $3,000 invested? The gain was taxed at ordinary income rates since the property was held less than six months but the income was "sheltered" with an apartment project on which I am taking fast depreciation.

Parcel Number	Size of Parcel (Acres)	Date Sold	Selling Price	Purchase Date	Purchase Price	Contemplated Use by Purchaser	Gross Profit
[1]1	1	7/72	$ 25,000	5/72	$ 16,000	Multi-family Dwelling	$ 9,000
2	2.8	11/72	20,500	11/69	12,500	Warehouse	8,000
3	25	1/73	40,000	10/69	20,000	Mobile Home Park	20,000
[2]4	13.56	6/73	39,000	3/71	5,000	Multi-family Dwelling	34,000
[3]5	51.58	6/73	165,000	6/73	125,000	Industrial	40,000
				Total Gross Profits			$111,000
				Less Gross Profits to Partners			– 37,000
				Gross Profits to the Author			$ 74,000

[1] This was joint venture with a partner. My share was 50 per cent.
[2] This was also 50-50 joint venture.
[3] Another joint venture. My share of ownership was 60 per cent.

Parcels No. 1 and No. 3 were sold for cash. Parcel No. 2 was sold with a small down payment and monthly payments for 23 months with the entire amount coming due on the 24th month. The note was secured by a trust deed on the property. Parcel No. 2 was purchased for cash; thus, I received no leveraging benefits. Parcel No. 3 was purchased with 25 per cent down and monthly notes on the balance at no interest.

Parcel No. 4 was residual land from a larger tract purchased for an apartment project. This property was traded for two first mortgage notes secured by deeds of trust on two residential houses and lots. Parcel No. 5 was bought and sold on the same date and the only cash investment by my partner and me was $10,000 in earnest money deposited on February 5, 1973. The purchase was for cash–however, by arranging the purchase and sale on the same date, the cash for our purchase was provided by the party to whom we sold the land.

While the purchase and sale were made the same day at a good profit, many months of work had gone into negotiations with numerous heirs located in several states.

I See By The Journal

Property Transfers
Carter-Glass Assoc. Inc. to James R. Diehnett, $39,000. District 9.
Glen F. Nicely to Marteq Corp., $165,000, District 8.
Margaret Knott Farrell and others to Glenn F. Nicely, $125,000, District 8.
Edward B. Rhegness to Alfred Green Sr., $15,000, District 2.
Walter Harvey Gibson to Kyle N. Hamilton, $28,500, District 6.

From the Knoxville Journal, Knoxville, Tennessee, June 27, 1973.

My great interest in raw property arises from my own experience and the results of my friends. I do not know anyone who has dealt consistently in this type of real estate in the last 30 years who has not made good money for his time and capital investments. I like it because it is where the profit is for the speculator, despite the fact that, when compared to improved property, it is more difficult to finance; it brings you no income until it is sold, and in slow periods or recessions it will be hit first and hardest.

Assuming you started in 1972 with $3,000 in capital and can double your money every four years, here is how your initial investment will grow:

1972	–	$ 3,000
1976	–	6,000
1980	–	12,000
1984	–	24,000
1988	–	48,000
1992	–	96,000
1996	–	192,000

My projections are in terms of *current* dollars which means that inflation has contributed to your total dollar gain. In other words, it is not likely that a 1980 dollar will have as much real value as a 1972 dollar. The foregoing does not take into account income taxes which would be imposed on your earnings nor does it consider the fact that you would not make all sales for cash.

Conversely, we have not considered leveraging, or the possibility of adding to your real estate capital account from savings, which could accelerate your pace enormously. For example, if with your $3,000 in cash in 1972 you could leverage your money by a small down payment and purchase $12,000 worth of property, which you could finish paying for in three or four years from savings, the projection would change thus:

1972	–	$ 12,000
1976	–	24,000
1980	–	48,000
1984	–	96,000
1988	–	192,000
1992	–	384,000
1996	–	768,000

From a practical viewpoint few, if any, would actually accomplish so great a pyramiding effect since some profits would likely be used for improving living standards and the full amount would not be available for reinvestment.

The returns on a $3,000 and $12,000 deposit in a bank or savings and loan association at 5 per cent interest compounded annually would be as follows:

1972	–	$3,000.00	1972	–	$12,000.00
1976	–	3,646.50	1976	–	14,586.00
1980	–	4,432.50	1980	–	17,730.00
1984	–	5,387.80	1984	–	21,551.20
1988	–	6,548.70	1988	–	26,194.80
1992	–	7,959.90	1992	–	31,839.60
1996	–	9,675.30	1996	–	38,701.20

6

WHAT TO BUY

Any time you find property not being put to its highest and best use there may be opportunity for profit. Losses have occurred infrequently on speculative real estate in recent years. Sometimes the profit must be postponed and is less than anticipated.

The alert and knowledgeable speculator does not buy just any piece of property that offers opportunity for profits. He keeps sifting until he has found the property which he believes to offer an opportunity for greater than normal profit in a short period of time.

Years ago, Theodore Roosevelt advised that "every person who invests in well-selected real estate in a growing section of a prosperous community adopts the surest and safest method of becoming independent, for real estate is the basis of wealth."

Real estate is never static. Business districts are continually shifting. Almost every major city has seen, or is now experiencing, the shifting of its central district. Actually, the trend is toward decentralization of the business district. The speculator, who can recognize a promising new district about to blossom out, can reap rewards. He must also recognize when a competitive district is opening up. Watch out for economic decay when making an investment. You may be tempted by unusually high yields on property approaching economic obsolescence.

Why Buy

The sound reasons for a speculator buying any property can be narrowed down to a few basics. Here they are:

1. The property is underpriced.
2. You foresee transitions in the area in the near future which will enhance the value of the property.
3. You believe the value can be increased by changing its appearance or subdividing and selling in smaller parcels.
4. You can have it rezoned to a higher use—making it more valuable.
5. You have a specific use, or know someone who does, who will pay more than your cost.

These pretty well cover the reasons for making a speculative purchase. Any one may be sufficient reason to buy or you may rely on a combination of several.

Purely from an investor's standpoint, there are others. The investor may be seeking a hedge against inflation, tax advantages, or a return on investment better than that received on a savings account. Unlike the speculator, he may be satisfied to own property netting 7 or 8 per cent annually, or if it is not income property, he may be satisfied to have his values keep pace with inflation.

The Best Buys (Sleepers)

Over the long haul, the investor must rely on paying current market prices for property but outguessing both the seller and other buyers as to future worth. There are situations, however, where you can buy property below the fair market price and expect to make a profit in a matter of days or weeks.

Bargain Situations

Generally, these situations are brought about by one of the following circumstances:

1. The owner is extremely dissatisfied with the property.
2. You have found a *sleeper*. The owner has not kept up with the market and will sell for less than value.
3. The property is about to come under the favorable influence of outside factors, such as a new highway, new factory, shopping center, and so forth.

Good Buy—Quick Profit

A few years ago I noticed a vacant house about three blocks from where I lived. The house was in a good neighborhood and about three years old. A realtor friend of mine had a sign on the property, and I stopped by his office to get the details.

The house was owned by Argonaut Realty Company, a division of General Motors, and was priced at $19,800. Argonaut had acquired the house from a General Motors employee under a plan whereby a transferred employee is protected from losing money on his home when he is transferred and has to sell.

I considered the asking price above market value and informed my friend that I had no interest in the property at that price. Several months went by and the sign remained. I again stopped by the office of my realtor friend and inquired if the price had changed. It had not, but he informed me that he was being pushed to sell it and invited me to make an offer.

We drove to the property and I looked it over. Room arrange-ment was good and construction sound. Improper grading of th back yard was permitting water to run under the house and stan in puddles, not a serious matter—easy to correct—but enough t frighten an inexperienced young couple about to buy their firs home.

We arrived back at his office, and I made him a $13,000 cas offer.

"They wouldn't consider a price that low," he said.

I insisted he call Argonaut and relay my offer which he did afte some persuading and finally realizing that this was my top offe

He made the call and was informed that they considered th offer extremely low but would discuss it and call back th afternoon. To his surprise they accepted the offer and informe him that they were mailing necessary information for closin

Within a week I received an offer of $15,500 on the house from a party that did not require financing. I arranged a joint closing, from Argonaut to me, and from me to the new party. I never used one penny of my money and cleared $2,500 less perhaps $100 in legal and recording fees.

The purpose of this illustration is to point out that circumstances sometimes determine whether an offer is ridiculous. You need to analyze each situation and use good judgment, however, since a person who is not particularly interested in selling can take offense at an extremely low offer.

Another Quick Turnover

I bought another bargain house from a friend who had backed his son in building it. He had already taken a beating in financing the construction as a result of his son's neglect of the project.

The purchase was initiated by a call from my friend who insisted that I make an offer. I refrained from offering a bargain price but he suggested a price so low that I could not refuse, and I told him he was selling too cheap. He acknowledged this fact, but said he was "sick of the venture" and wanted to wash it out. As in the other illustration, I immediately sold the house for a good profit without even taking title in my name or using a dime of my own money.

My First Venture

On another occasion, my first speculative land venture, I made an offer on a new house and 60 acres of land through an attorney who told me that he would submit the offer as a favor to me, but he was almost sure his client, who had moved away, wouldn't consider accepting my price. His client had just received title to the property after long and bitter litigation. To the attorney's surprise, he received a telegram in response to my offer accepting same and informing us a representative would be in our town in two days to close the deal.

Since I had made a cash offer, I had to do some scrambling to raise the cash on such short notice but managed to work it out and in the meantime got a sales contract from an adjoining farmer for 45 acres of the land for nearly enough to pay for the entire property.

The Once in a Lifetime Opportunity

If you decide to become a serious dabbler in real estate, keep your eyes open for that rare opportunity to hit the *big lick*. The first challenge is recognizing the opportunity; the second will likely be financing it. If your resources are modest, you will need to use all of the ingenuity at your command. (You may find some ideas in our chapter on "Leverage.")

During the early 1960's I was in the real estate brokerage and insurance business along with two partners.

A new by-pass around our town of 15,000 population had been in the talking and planning stages for several years, and the time was drawing near when it would be built. We secured a six months option on about 30 acres of land for $65,000, but progress on the proposed by-pass was slow, and we did not have a prospective purchaser as our option neared expiration. Our firm did not have sufficient funds to exercise the cash option and we relinquished our rights to a partner who made a joint venture with a money partner who could afford to put up the purchase price and wait for the by-pass to develop. Shortly, thereafter, I sold my interest in the real estate brokerage business and moved to another city.

Last fall, ten years later, I ran across my ex-partner and inquired how he made out on the property. He and his financial partner had already sold more than a half million dollars worth of highway frontage and had half of the original acreage left. The by-pass had given them several thousand feet of valuable commercial frontage. Obviously our firm, which originally optioned the property, thought it was a good buy. We failed, however, to recognize its real potential, else we would have made the necessary sacrifices to swing the financing. The necessary capital can usually be found if the deal has real merit.

Front End Profit

A short time ago, two partners and I optioned some land and made a proposal on a several million dollar housing project. Ou proposal was accepted. We ran into zoning problems and were forced to come up with another site. We had spent considerable money in options, engineering, core drilling and preliminary architectural plans. Rather than overextend ourselves and risk losing the project, we approached the head of a company with greater resources, who was developing similar type projects.

A joint venture arrangement was worked out which guaranteed us close to a quarter of a million dollars. Our joint venture partner made more than a million, but they had the capital and were willing to take the risks on a project which required nearly three years to complete.

Selling to a Developer

Based upon experience, the cost of raw land is usually not the determining factor as to where a developer locates a subdivision since land represents a small portion of the building cost. Grading, filling, drainage, and utilities may account for 70 to 80 per cent of the developed land price. The fact that the raw land accounts for a small percentage of the total price is to the advantage of the speculator.

For example, let's assume you are selling a developer 10 acres of land for $25,000 which he can develop into 25 lots and subsequently construct speculative houses on the lots.

His developed land costs may be near the following:

Land	$ 25,000
Street, utilities, and other land development costs	75.000
Cost of developed land	$100,000 = $4,000 per lot

Assume the cost of building single family residences average $30,000 each—making a combined land, development, building cost of $34,000.

Land cost per lot	$ 1,000
Improvements per lot	3,000
Structures per lot	30,000
	$34,000

Land cost is less than 3 per cent of the total. Suppose now, that you had increased the price of the land by 50 per cent, charging the developer $37,500 and making his raw land cost $1,500 per lot. The precentage of the total package represented by land would only increase by about 1½ per cent.

CHEAP PROPERTY

A few individuals have the knack of buying, selling, and renting cheap property. There seems to be one or more individuals in almost every community who specializes in this type of real estate.

The investment is low–the return is good–and the *headaches* are many.

I have never dealt extensively in this type of real estate but am acquainted with numerous people who have. Some have accumulated considerable wealth.

Quite often these individuals are characterized as slum landlords, and under the normal concept of the term, there is a stigma attached. Undoubtedly, some are unethical, but most are honorable and straight forward business men and women with a particular aptitude for handling old and "run down" property and doing business with low income people.

To succeed in cheap property you must be firm and aggressive. A softie could not survive in this business. You can get higher than average return on your money, but you will earn it.

Demands High Return

One woman with whom I am acquainted owns more than 50 cheap properties–single family residence, duplexes, and apartments. Many of these were acquired with a few hundred dollars equity money and assuming loans which she amortizes over a relatively short period (about 10 years average) out of rental payments. She usually disposes of the property after all or most of the depreciation is used and the property no longer offers any tax advantages.

She will not buy property where the anticipated return is less than 18 per cent and this is calculated with a liberal allowance for contingencies–repairs, vacancies, default in rent, and so forth. Some of her properties have an annual gross of 50 per cent of her purchase prices and in extreme cases she has grossed in excess of 100 per cent of the cost the first year.

"Ground Rules" for Success

The real secret is in buying property that requires very few repairs since the high cost of labor and materials usually makes it impossible to come out with a good investment after major repairs.

Ready cash is a must for dealing in cheap property. Often it is acquired from an estate with the heirs wanting to cash out. Many times the seller is in distressed financial circumstances and needs cash quickly. His equity may be small—often less than $500.

Rents must be collected promptly and sometimes firmly. A tenant who gets a month behind may never be able to catch up. Watch out for undesirable tenants. Screen them carefully and get the highest deposit possible.

If your phone rings a lot at night, just remember you could have put your money in a savings and loan without any bother, but at only 5 per cent interest. You are working for 15 or 20 or even a 30 per cent return. If you happen to be handy with tools, this is a plus. One visit from a plumber can cost a month's rent.

Learn to recognize real hardships as opposed to perpetual hard luck stories. Whether you like it or not you may wind up as landlord, banker, and confessor to your tenants.

DISTRESS PROPERTY

Often good leverage can be combined with a bargain price on property which is on the brink of foreclosure. Many times property in distress may have a bright future, but the owner has overextended himself and cannot meet current obligations, and the property is heavily mortgaged in proportion to today's market value; else it would not be in distress.

Lending institutions usually only foreclose as a last resort. Foreclosure proceedings are expensive. Property in foreclosure often brings less than it is worth—many times forcing the lending institution to bid it in to protect its interest, and lending institutions do not relish the publicity surrounding foreclosures.

In view of the foregoing, a purchaser can often get excellent terms on the property.

Leveraging on Distressed Property

A friend of mine purchased a major chain motel licensed to a franchisee a few years ago. The owner was in default on the mortgage payments–behind many installments amounting to a huge sum of money. The lender first insisted that my friend pay all of the past due installments. When he refused, the lender agreed to accept payment of all past due interest, and to defer the principal payments in arrears. The purchase was made, new management installed, and a loser was turned into a very profitable business by a new owner who acquired a million dollars worth of real estate–using virtually no capital. The point here is that the buyer was able to use a distress situation for leverage–acquiring the property for delinquent interest payments, whereas, on a new loan the lender would have demanded perhaps 25 per cent equity money.

Property in distress is not always a good buy. The mortgage amount may be greater than actual worth. When this situation occurs it is often on residential property which we do rank high for speculation.

MAKING PROFITABLE CHOICES

When considering the types of property in which I would invest, I rate close-in tracts or acreage at the top of the list. Land which has commercial or industrial potentials is the very best, but land with residential subdivision possibilities can also be very desirable–particularly if it lends itself to use for high density multi-family housing.

Commercial and industrial lots may also offer great profit potential but may be expensive to inventory due to high initial cost and high tax assessment. Also, I have found it difficult to leverage satisfactorily on this type of property when the owner demands cash, and money must be acquired through a lending institution. Sometimes the owner's willingness to accept a small down payment and carry the balance will solve this problem.

Residential Lots

I do not generally look upon single family residential lots as attractive buys. This is particularly true when buying a lot or lots in a large new subdivision. There is a great chance that the subdivision developer will be your competitor for two or three years or more. In all likelihood as the subdivision develops you will be able to realize a profit on your lot—but the potential is not great.

Sometimes you can find a *sleeper* lot or small tract in an older part of town which can be cleaned up and marketed at a good profit—particularly if it has multifamily possibilities.

Farmland

I do not rate farmland where future contemplated use is farming very high. The average value of farmland has been increasing at a rate of 5 or 6 per cent nationally in recent years; although, in 1972 this shot up to 10 per cent nationwide with some states reflecting more than a 20 per cent average increase.

In recent years there has been a growing market in cheap farmland and woodland—often mountain tracts. This is being purchased for hunting and fishing camps, second homes, weekend retreats, a hedge against inflation, and so forth. Reports from some states indicate that more than half of the sales of farmland is being made to nonfarmers, and often most of these are from metropolitan areas a great distance away.

When I refer to cheap land, I am usually thinking of $50 an acre or less and certainly not more than $100 an acre. A few years ago cheap land may have indicated a range of $10 to $30 an acre, but with greater demand and inflation, these prices are practically nonexistent, and the areas where land can be purchased for $50 an acre are very limited.

Whether or not this extensive market in cheap farmland by city dwellers will be sustained or increased is anybody's guess. With the mounting problems of the congested cities, coupled with continuing inflation and shorter work weeks, it appears to have a good chance to continue. Undoubtedly, this type of market will always soften early in recessions, when budgets get tighter, usually accompanied by an added emotional effect of conservatism including a reluctance to go in debt for anything other than absolute necessities.

Opportunities Summarized

In summary of the foregoing I would rate the more common categories of vacant land based on opportunities for profit in the following order:

1. Tracts and acreage (including farms) suitable for subdivision.
2. Commercial or industrial lots.
3. Small lots or parcels for multifamily use in a mature section of the city. Just below this would be the same type of property but restricted to single family use.
4. Cheap remote acreage suitable for recreational purposes such as hunting and fishing camps, weekend retreats, summer homes, and so forth. Many of these parcels have an old dwelling house and other improvements which are worth the entire asking price–assuming use can be established for them.
5. Farms where highest potential is farming.
6. Single family residential lots in new subdivisions.

The foregoing preferences are based on experience and observations. Many may disagree. Certainly thousands of exceptions could be cited. You will develop your own preferences and opinions as you get experience in buying and selling.

HOME OWNERSHIP–WISE OR FOOLISH?

Whether to buy or rent your own home–for those who have a choice–is an old unsettled argument.

From an economic standpoint the pros and cons are about equally divided. Houses, however, to most families mean more than a shelter against the elements; they become homes which are the center of family social activities where children are reared and characters are molded. For these reasons any logical discussion on owning versus renting must embrace more than the consideration of money costs.

Advantages of Home Ownership

More specifically, a few of the advantages of home ownership, aside from the economics of ownership, include:

1. *Inducement to save.* Many people cannot discipline themselves to accumulate money or equities without a schedule obligation.
2. *Credit.* Banks and other lending institutions generally look upon home ownership as an indication of stability.
3. *Security.* If you are a tenant in a single family house, the landlord may at anytime decide to sell or occupy the house himself. Rarely would you be protected by more than a one year lease. In an apartment your rent may be raised beyond your means. Also, even though your payments may be amortized over 20 or 30 years, it gives you added peace of mind to believe it will ultimately be paid for.
4. *Citizenship.* Since the value of your home will be influenced by the quality of schools, streets, utilities, police protection, and so forth, your interest in public affairs will be keener. George Washington once said, "Strongly I am impressed with the beneficial effects which our country would receive if every good citizen of the United States owned his own home."
5. *Adding to value.* Many home owners convert a part of their leisure time to value through such activities as landscaping or adding on a room. For the office or factory worker these can be "fun" things as well as profitable.

Home Ownership at an Earlier Age

With present day big loan to value ratios most families can now achieve home ownership at an early age, whereas a generation or two back home ownership usually required years of sacrifice and savings.

One thing that keeps the single family housing market strong is a belief on the part of the buyers that it is almost impossible to lose on this investment and statistics for recent years indicate buyers with this attitude have been right much more often than wrong. The main exception is a house in a declining neighborhood and in some instances a home in a community where a major industry has closed down.

In prime sectors of many cities, however, increases in value at rates from 5 to 15 per cent annually have not been unusual—many have been higher.

Housing Costs

According to the Department of Labor, home ownership costs rose by 38.8 per cent in the five year period 1966-1971. Scarcity of desirable land has been a big factor in this increase. The average lot for FHA insured single family residences rose 44 per cent for the five year period ending in 1972, and building costs increased at an even greater rate during the same period.

If your ambition is keeping up with the Joneses, you might be interested to know, according to HUD and the Department of Commerce, the median sales price for single family houses rose from $18,000 in 1963 to $25,200 in 1971. Only 4 per cent of the home buyers were able to purchase a residence for under $15,000 in 1970, the same percentage which were willing to pay more than $50,000.

Most housing units were renter-occupied from 1900 through the 1940's. Now, however, homeowners outnumber those who pay rent to landlords by nearly two to one.

The High Costs of Owning

The preceding presents most of the bright side of home ownership. Now perhaps we should look at some of the sacrifices in the form of expenses and costs which a homeowner must endure.

Many homeowners are surprised to find that paying rent wasn't as bad as they thought, once they start meeting the real costs of owning and operating a home.

The one big break which owners in recent years have received has been appreciation in value. While automobiles, appliances, furniture, and so forth become much less valuable each year due to wearing out, houses have been appreciating. Even so, the costs of ownership are much higher than the uninitiated surmise. Among these are:

1. Closing costs when purchasing.
2. Foregoing interest or income on down payment or equity.
3. Interest on mortgage.
4. Maintenance and repairs.
5. Property taxes.
6. Special assessments.
7. Hazard and liability insurance.

One Example

To get an example of the real costs of owning a home, I conferred with an owner who purchased a house in a suburb of a city of 35,000 population ten years ago.

Purchase price of the house was $30,000, including closing costs. A conventional loan of $23,000 was obtained through an insurance company for a period of 25 years at an interest rate of 5½ per cent (about 3 per cent below today's market).

His monthly payments for principal, interest, insurance, and taxes are $226.52. The payments are higher today than in the earlier years due to increase in cost of taxes and insurance which will likely further increase over the period of the loan, but we will consider these payments average.

In addition to expenses included in monthly payments, his other real costs are estimated as follows:

Maintenance	$ 25.00	per month
Income foregone on equity based on 5 per cent return (not compounded) on $7,000	29.17	
Utilities (heating, cooling, water, and sewer)	45.00	
	$ 99.17	Expenses not included in loan

$ 99.17	
226.52	Monthly loan payments
$325.69	Total
71.33	Average monthly payback on principal ($23,000 divided by 300 months = $71.33)
$254.36	Monthly cost of owning home.

$254.36 x 300 months (period of loan) = $76,208.00 - cost of home ownership for 25 years.

Utilities are not technically a cost of homeownership; however, including their costs here may make comparisons with rentals, where utilities are sometimes furnished easier. Under most accounting procedures an item would be included for depreciation. Based on accelerating replacement costs, it is doubtful whether there is any real dollar depreciation—thus the item is omitted.

Lending institutions generally feel that the original cost of a home should not exceed two to two and one-half times the buyers annual income.

For further reading on homeownership, I recommend Real Estate Principles and Practices by Alfred A. Ring and Nelson L. North, Prentice-Hall, Inc., Englewood Cliffs, New Jersey.

TOTAL RENT PAID OVER A 25 YEAR PERIOD

At $100.00 per month

In 5 years	$ 6,000
In 10 years	12,000
In 15 years	18,000
In 20 years	24,000
In 25 years	30,000

At $150.00 per month

In 5 years	$ 9,000
In 10 years	18,000
In 15 years	27,000
In 20 years	36,000
In 25 years	45,000

At $200.00 per month

In 5 years	$ 12,000
In 10 years	24,000
In 15 years	36,000
In 20 years	48,000
In 25 years	60,000

At $250.00 per month

In 5 years	$ 15,000
In 10 years	30,000
In 15 years	45,000
In 20 years	60,000
In 25 years	75,000

At $300.00 per month

In 5 years	$ 18,000
In 10 years	36,000
In 15 years	54,000
In 20 years	72,000
In 25 years	90,000

AMOUNT REQUIRED TO AMORTIZE A 25 YEAR LOAN AT 7½ PER CENT INTEREST

(Taxes and Insurance not included)

$10,000.00 house loan	$22,170
15,000.00 house loan	33,255
20,000.00 house loan	44,340
25,000.00 house loan	55,425
30,000.00 house loan	66,510
40,000.00 house loan	88,680
50,000.00 house loan	110,850

How to Gain on Your Home Mortgage

If you are borrowing money to buy a home—shop for the best loan possible. Some factors making a favorable loan include low down payment, long amortization term, favorable interest rate, small discount, prepayment option, and reasonable closing costs.

Try to get the highest possible loan to value ratio because this will be an advantage if you resell your home during the first few years of the loan. Your purchaser can likely apply for and receive a new loan, but closing costs and discounts are expensive. Therefore, an existing loan which the purchaser can assume after paying for your equity will usually make your house easier to sell. If you follow the national average pattern you will sell your house within five or six years from the date of purchase.

In the early years of the mortgage your monthly interest cost will be several times as much as your principal repayment. If you contemplate living in your home until the loan is fully paid you may want to consider accelerating your principal payments.

Should you have a HUD or VA mortgage you can prepay some of your principal when you have extra funds. Some conventional lenders permit prepayment, others may only allow prepayment without penalty after the first five or ten years.

VA requests prepayment in exact principal amounts, according to the loan schedule. Others specify minimum amounts or "even" dollar prepayments. Some will take any reasonable amount and apply to the principal.

Let's assume you have borrowed $25,000 for a period of 25 years (300 months) at an interest rate of 7¾ per cent, with the first installment due January 1, 1974. Monthly installments are $179.11 and you have paid the first eight installments and are now ready to make your September 1974 payment.

PAYMENT DATE	INTEREST	PRINCIPAL	LOAN BALANCE
September 1974	$160.53	$18.58	$24,836.95
October 1974	160.41	18.70	24,818.25
November 1974	160.28	18.83	24,799.42

If you will include your October principal payment of $18.70 with your regular September installment you will eleminate on full month's interest of more than $160.00. Your next payment i made on the regular due date, but you will be skipping th October payment and paying the November installment. By takin advantage of this situation when you have extra cash you ma shorten your loan many months or many years and save severa thousand dollars in interest charges.

7

LEVERAGE

If your goal is to make a lot of money in real estate, the single most important consideration is leverage or the realization of the maximum potential on cash used.

Maximum leverage and maximum security are not always compatible, and you must make a choice whether your goal is maximum leverage or maximum security or some place in between.

Without the use of leverage, profits (or losses) from real estate investments will generally relate to the size of the investment. The man who buys a $2,000 residential lot, sells it for $4,000, has made the same percentage return as the man who buys a $100,000 commercial lot and sells for $200,000. There is, however, a $98,000 difference in the before tax profits.

Leverage is usually obtained by one of two methods:

1. Long term options.
2. Low down payments–and long time amortization.

Two Good Leverage Deals

Structuring a deal for great leverage requires imagination and resourcefullness.

Two friends of mine have used great leverage over and over with absolutely beautiful results.

A few years ago they obtained a long-time lease on a farm bordered by a main highway on the north side of a small city in which expansion was fairly dormant at the time but with clear cut signs that when growth started it would be on the north side of town.

The lease was obtained from a school teacher and part-time farmer who had no interest in development and was glad to receive a monthly income much greater than could be anticipated from farming the land.

The lease price was $300 a month. Within three years they transferred their lease to a shopping center developer for $96,000. This is *leverage.*

These same men optioned an 80 acre farm in the same city for $1,000 an acre. The option was for five years with modest monthly payments–about enough for taxes and a conservative interest return on the $80,000 asking price.

Five years brought a lot of changes–sewers to the area, proposed new roads, and so forth. A short time before the option expired, they sold 40 acres (half of the property) for $3,000 an acre–paid the owner his $80,000–reimbursed themselves for expenses (about $10,000)–had $30,000 and 40 acres as profits. Most of the remaining land has now been disposed of, some for as much as $10,000 an acre. This is *leverage.*

How could deals like this have been made? Not by accident! The owner had not listed their property nor offered it for sale under these terms and conditions.

First of all, my speculator friends had to recognize the worth of the property–*tomorrow,* not today. Secondly, they had to correctly analyze the posture of the owners. They had to determine what would be acceptable to the owners besides a lot of cash, which my friends did not have.

Don't take too much for granted. Most speculators with limited capital would have missed these deals. These men substituted imagination for capital. Don't rely on what you think the average person would do with a piece of property. Try to analyze the owner's position and how he thinks. Most of your good purchases will be made from older people and your sales will be to younger people. Many owners, particularly older ones, don't want to be bothered with the complexities of subdivision or development

Sometimes there are numerous heirs which make any action, other than outright optioning, selling, or leasing the entire tract, complicated. Some people are literally frightened out of their wits by the thought of being annexed and having to pay higher taxes.

Increased Taxes—Owner Panics

I knew an elderly widow who had a nice farm just outside the city limits of a growing small town.

Many persons approached her about the possibility of purchasing the land, but she would not even discuss it. Then the city annexed the farm. This meant higher taxes, but it also meant lower insurance rates, garbage pick-up, water, sewer, and so forth.

Her one thought, however, was of the increased taxes, and she turned the property over to an auction firm who subdivided it and sold it. Had she waited two or three years, she would have received two or three times more money.

Need Income—Not Ready to Sell

There may be a house and large lot in your town with terrific commercial potential. The traffic and noise are already making it undesirable for a residence, but the couple living there are taking care of the wife's 89-year-old invalid mother and would not consider a move which would be upsetting to her. They may, however, need extra income. They might consider a five-year option at a very reasonable price, if they could receive $300 a month income.

Use your imagination—be resourceful.

More Leverage—More Risk

You have $10,000 to invest. You can buy a $10,000 piece of property and pay for it. Little risk, no leverage. You can buy a $30,000 piece of property and pay $5,000 or $10,000 down. More risk, more leverage. You can get a year's option for the same money on a $100,000 piece of property which may be worth $200,000 in a year. Lots of risk, lots of leverage.

Leveraging Opportunities Greatest in Real Estate

Down payments on real estate of under 30 per cent are quite common, and many transactions take place with from 10 to 20 per cent down. Often the purchaser can finance the balance over a period of five to ten years with the owner carrying the balance on a note secured only by a first mortgage on the property.

This kind of leverage is difficult to get in any other type of investment. Certainly you cannot approach this in dealing in common stocks. Margin requirements which are controlled by the Securities Exchange Commission now stand at 65 per cent.

While we are comparing a regulated with an unregulated situation, it is obvious that the risk factor is much less in real estate than in common stocks.

Let's assume you know an individual who owns 500 shares of Litton Industries. He is willing to sell at the market price and you are willing to buy, but you only have 20 per cent of the purchase price and want to pay off the balance over five years with monthly installments and going bank rate interest, with the stock as your only security.

The seller would not consider these terms, but the same individual might sell you a farm or a commercial lot for 20 per cent down with five years to pay the balance. The difference is in the *quality* of the security.

Properly applied, leverage can enable you to make profits far out of proportion of the amount of your investment.

No Interest Leveraging

I bought 25 acres of woodland which had residential subdivision possibilities a few years ago. The owner was an elderly gentleman and his asking price was $25,000. After several conferences he agreed to take $20,000. I offered $18,000 cash and he refused. I then countered with an offer to meet his $20,000 price if he would accept $5,000 down and a *balloon* note with maturity in two years–monthly payments of $150 and no interest. He accepted the offer. I considered the purchase under these terms equivalent, or better than, the $18,000 cash offer and the owner was satisfied since he only needed a small amount of cash and the property was not bringing him any income.

Many Option Possibilities

Most owners will only grant options for a short duration. Occasionally you can get an option for one dollar but usually the owner will require 1 or 2 per cent of the purchase price which you will forfeit if you fail to exercise the option.

Often, however, you can get a much longer option by posting a much larger amount and if you are sure you want to buy the property and will be in position to make the required financial arrangements, this may be a good approach. For example, you are interested in a $50,000 parcel of property. The owner might grant you a short option for one dollar or not more than $500 or $1,000. If you are not ready to use the property, why not counter with an offer of $10,000 for a one- or two-year option, with the $10,000 to be applied to purchase price? Holding a $50,000 piece of property for two years will cost you about $8,000 in interest paid or foregone.

There are many situations where the full amount of cash is required to make a purchase. When you purchase on this basis try to offset the lost leveraging effects by buying at the lowest possible price. Even when the owner has signed a contract of agreeing to accept a small down payment and a note, you may want to consider offering him an alternative of cash—but at a lower price.

Keep Reserves in Time and Money

Be careful never to let your cash reserves and/or ability to borrow become too limited. When you are depending on the sale of property you own to pay for property which you are buying allow plenty of time. Most transactions require more—not less—time than you anticipate. Most improvements to property will cost more—not less—than you estimate.

8

SUBDIVIDING RESIDENTIAL LAND

Migration from the inner-city to suburbia has made subdivisions of raw land a profitable business for many speculators.

For the beginning speculator, lacking experience and with limited spare time, I recommend leaving subdividing and speculative building to the seasoned developer. As you gain experience, land subdivision is an undertaking in which you can profitably engage on a spare-time basis.

Reasons for Demand

Properly selected and developed, subdivided residential land usually sells well for one or both of the following reasons:

1. There is a genuine need for residential lots by speculative builders and by families planning to build a home.
2. There are many individuals who like to speculate in lots as a hedge against inflation and in the hopes of increased values as homes are built on other lots in the new subdivision. (I do not consider developed residential lots to be the best buys for speculators, nevertheless, they are in great demand in many areas.)

My experience has led me to believe the best opportunities for residential subdivisions are in areas where a minimum of local governmental regulations apply.

For example, if you are located in a county or municipality

which requires 25 or 30 feet paved and guttered streets, underground utilities, and so forth, you should leave subdivision in this area to an experienced full-time developer. Cost overruns will likely erode your profits if the job does not have close supervision. Even if you have the time, proper supervision requires a great amount of knowledge and experience which you do not have if you are a beginner.

Factors Affecting Profit

There are at least five factors which will effect the profit you make on a subdivision as follows:

1. The price of the raw land.
2. The cost of your improvements.
3. Length of time you have investment in the land.
4. Cost of selling.
5. Price received for developed lots.

Low Investment—High Return

The best percentage profit I ever experienced in subdividing raw land was on a parcel of land purchased in partnership with my brother in 1965. We bought 60 acres of mountain property for $6,000, or $100 an acre, near a rural community, close to a good highway, and only a few miles from the county seat. With the help of a "moonlighting" surveyor, who worked regularly for the Forest Service, we divided the parcel into 55 lots and a remaining tract of 30 acres. A few months after purchasing we held an auction sale and sold 13 lots for enough to recover our total land costs, our surveying work, grading and graveling streets, and installing a water line. The remaining 43 lots and 30 acre tract represented compensation for our time and profits.

I have handled numerous other "cheap land" subdivisions in a similar manner and at a satisfactory profit.

High Land Costs—Low Return

In contrast to the above, I purchased for a company which I once represented a tract of 20 acres for $4,000 an acre. The tract was located in a community with good demand for developed lots at from $4,000 to $6,000. It was a struggle to break even because of high administrative overhead; development standards set by the city in which it was located; changes of policy with the change of city administration during development; and an over design by an engineering firm which received a fee based on development costs.

Some Do's and Don'ts When Subdividing

Most semi-rural subdivisions rely on septic tanks and drain fields for sewage disposal. Where these are used it is essential that the soil have good percolation qualities which must usually be verified by state or local health officials. *Never, never* try to cheat on this factor, for to do so will only lead to grief down the road. Even if you do not open the door to expensive litigation, you will have violated the confidence which the lot buyers placed in you and a group of irate home owners having to pump out septic tanks will not enhance your future reputation as a developer.

Adequate amounts of water and good pressure are also essential. Don't try to get by with a three-inch line when your engineer says a four- or six-inch line is required for good service. Actually the cost of installing a six-inch line is little more than a three-inch line and particularly if you use plastic pipe, the cost of the larger pipe is very nominal. Running lateral water lines to lot corners is not a great expense and will preclude the necessity of tearing up the road bed each time a new house is tied on. Hidden extras such as these can usually be recovered in your lot prices, whether sales are made at auction or privately, if it is properly explained to the buyers.

Easiest to Handle

The easiest subdivision of all is on land with sufficient road frontage to permit you to cut out lots and tracts without building new roads. Many areas have a good demand for tracts, baby farms, or mini-farms of from three to ten acres. Road frontage which lends itself to this kind of development is becoming scarce and more expensive but many people have made good money in this manner and some are still doing it.

Buy Tract—Wholesale Subdivision

In the event that you live in a community where development standards are high and you do not have time, capital, or experience for total development—you may want to consider purchasing land, completing your surveying and engineering, recording your plat—then selling to a builder or developer. One word of caution about this approach. Often taxes will increase sharply once a subdivision plat is recorded and these could add considerably to the total costs of your property if you hold it for an extended period.

Leverage Possibilities

There is a possibility that you can leverage to a great advantage on a subdivision. Many property owners will take a small down payment—20 per cent or less—and agree to release individual lots as they are sold. You should strive to keep the amount required for lot releases as low as possible since you will need to sell some lots for small cash payments and accept notes on the balance. If you have to pay the original owner $3,000 to release a lot which you sell for $5,000 but only receive $1,500 in down payments, you will quickly run into cash flow problems. You may also be faced with the necessity of selling lots to builders and accepting personal notes so they can have clear title when mortgaging for construction loans. This is a common practice. Just make sure the builders are solvent and reliable. Your bank may agree to carry these notes for you, since they will usually run for a short time, often less than six months.

How to Proceed

After purchasing the raw land your first step will be to get an accurate survey made and have a plat drawn. If it is a large tract with severe grades you will need an accurate topographic map made of the property. This can be done with an aerial survey or with ground crews. On relatively level parcels you may use inexpensive "quad sheet" topos, available from local dealers or The U.S. Geological Survey at nominal costs. The scale on these is extremely small with vertical contours at 20 feet intervals. Even when blown up they are not adequate where a high degree of accuracy is required. One of the chief reasons for using accurate topos is to control grades and make full utilization of the land. Where land is relatively level and cheap expense may not be justified.

After you have acquired a topo map you may want to employ a land planner for laying out the subdivision on a plat, or an experienced engineer may be able to render this service as well as staking out your streets and utility lines.

Normally, the local electric company and local phone company will install service in the subdivision without cost to you, but they will need to set some of their poles on your property. Provide easements for these when you record your plat. Usually, if you provide utility companies with a copy of your preliminary plat they will point out where easements will be needed and your engineer can indicate these on the completed plat before recording. If you don't do this prior to selling, easements will have to be acquired from lot owners, and even if they are all cooperative, locating them and getting them to sign the necessary documents can be time-consuming. Underground utilities are preferred and even required in some areas. They are more expensive and usually this cost is borne by the developer.

Rough grading, smooth grading, ditching, drainage and graveling can usually be contracted at reasonable prices from small local contractors.

Don't Overdevelop

Regardless of how much land you acquire, do not develop and expose too many lots for sale at one time. If you think that 20 lots a year will saturate the demands in your community *don't develop 100,* else buyers will sense that you are overstocked on lots and will be in no hurry to buy.

Other Suggestions

Obviously, land that is level or rolling will be less expensive to develop than land with severe slopes when a lot of filling and cutting is required for your roads and streets. If blasting is required for roads or utilities, this is very expensive, so the cheapest raw land may not result in the lowest lot costs to you.

The size of your lots will depend somewhat on community demand and custom and may be further governed by local subdivision regulations or health department requirements where septic tanks and drain fields are used.

About 15,000 square feet is an average requirement where you are not served by a central sewer system. Some areas require 20,000 square feet or more–some require 10,000 or 12,000 square feet where the subdivision is served by a central water system and more if individual water wells are contemplated.

You should expect to get slightly more than two lots per acre where 15,000 square feet are required. An acre has 43,560 square feet but an allowance must be made for roads and streets and most areas require a 50 feet or 60 feet right-of-way, even though you may only "surface" 18 or 20 feet.

Where the property is served by sewers, lot sizes are usually smaller but here again you will be governed by local custom and/or local governmental regulations. In some areas sewered lots may be as large as 100 feet by 150 feet–in others, 25 feet by 100 feet may be acceptable.

Planning and zoning regulations may stipulate the required set back from the street right-of-way and side and back lot lines. Where no regulations govern, you should include reasonable requirements in your own deed restrictions.

It is important to record your subdivision restrictions, along with your plat, before the first lot is sold. Failure to properly restrict your subdivision can jeopardize the success of your subdivision. One shack or hog pen can deflate the value of 50 surrounding lots.

Your restrictions should be reasonable and in keeping with the neighborhood. Imposing restrictions which would have the effect of requiring $40,000 homes where the neighborhood average is $25,000 could cost you many sales.

When you subdivide and sell lots you will be taxed at ordinary income tax rates rather than capital gains rates.

The following restrictions were used on the subdivision to which I made earlier reference of recovering all cost on the sale of the first 13 lots:

Protective Covenants

"WHEREAS, the undersigned is the owner of a tract of land in the 11th Civil District of Carter County, Tennessee, which has been subdivided into what is known as the "White Pine Hills Subdivision," as shown by plat of said Subdivision of record in Plat Book 3, page 132, of the Register's Office for Carter County, Tennessee. And

WHEREAS, the undersigned desires to create an exclusive residential section by said subdivision.

NOW, THEREFORE, in consideration of the premises, and in order to protect the future development of said property and the future owners of lots in the White Pine Hills Subdivision, the following Protective Covenants are hereby adopted and made covenants running with the land, and shall be as binding upon the heirs, executors, administrators, and assigns of the present owners thereof as upon the present owner himself:

1. All lots in the Subdivision shall be known and designated as residential lots.
2. That no use of this land will be used for business or industrial purposes, nor will there be any detached dwellings erected but only conventional one family dwellings will be erected.
3. No building shall be located nearer the front lot line than 30 feet, or nearer the side lines of said lot than 15 feet, and any detached building shall be set back not less than 65 feet from the front lot line, or nearer than 15 feet to the side line.
4. No residential structure shall be erected or placed on any building lot, which plot has an area of less than 12,000 square feet or a width of less than 80 feet at the front building set back line, and only one residence on each lot.
5. Any residence or residential outbuilding shall be of first-class materials and workmanship. No dwelling shall be constructed entirely of cinder or concrete block. Block may be used in foundation, or inside of wall to veneer with brick.
6. No roof of corrugated tin or other metals shall be used on any residence erected on said property, except metal shingles are acceptable.

7. The ground floor area of the main structure of each dwelling, exclusive of one story open porches and garage, shall not be less than 1,000 square feet in the case of a one story structure, nor less than 1,250 square feet in the case of a one and one-half, two, or two and one-half story structure.

8. No trailer, basement, tent, shack, garage, barn, or other outbuildings erected in the subdivision shall at any time be used as a residence, temporarily or permanently, nor shall any structure, either temporary or permanent in character, be erected in the subdivision, the primary purpose of which is usage as a garage, unless such structure conforms, in general, with the main residence erected on the plot.

9. No noxious or offensive trade or activity shall be carried on upon any lot, nor shall anything be done thereon which may be or become an annoyance or nuisance to the neighborhood. No hog pens or raising of hogs is allowed.

10. Until such time as a sanitary sewer system shall have been installed to serve this addition, a sewage disposal system constructed in accordance with the requirements of the State Board of Health shall be installed to serve each dwelling. The affluent from septic tanks shall not be permitted to discharge into a stream, storm sewer, open ditch or drain unless it has first passed through an absorption field.

11. No lot shall be used or maintained as a dumping ground for rubbage. Trash, garbage or other waste shall not be kept except in sanitary containers. All incinerators or other equipment for the storage or disposal of such material shall be kept in a clean and sanitary condition.

If the party hereto, or his heirs and assigns, shall violate or attempt to violate any of the covenants herein, it shall be lawful for any other person or persons owning any real property situated in said development or subdivision to prosecute any proceedings at law or in equity against the person or persons violating or attempting to violate any such covenant and either to prevent him or them from so doing or recover damages or other dues for such violation.

These covenants shall take effect immediately, and invalidation of any one of these covenants by judgment or Court order shall in no wise affect any of the other provisions which shall remain in full force and effect.

IN WITNESS WHEREOF, the undersigned has hereunto set his hand and seal on this the 18 day of August, 1965.

Glen Nicely

STATE OF TENNESSEE
COUNTY OF CARTER

Personally appeared before me, the undersigned authority, a Notary

Public in and for said State and County, and within named bargainer, Glen Nicely, with whom I am personally acquainted, and who acknowledged that he executed the within instrument for the purposes therein contained.

WITNESS my hand and official seal at office, this the 18 day of August, 1965.

My Commission Expires: February 4, 1968.

Edna Hicks
NOTARY PUBLIC

STATE OF TENNESSEE, CARTER COUNTY
REGISTER'S OFFICE

Received for Record the 18th day of August, A.D. Nineteen Hundred and 65 at 10:50 o'clock a.m., Noted in Note Book 12 Page 377, and recorded in Book of Deeds Misc., Vol. 21 Page 57.

A.H. Hardin
REGISTER

Protecting the Environment

The speculator must keep in mind that more and more future development will have to be in harmony with environmental considerations. Land values will be vitally affected by legislation at all levels of government relating to clean air, clean water, and freedom from pollution.

With the acute awareness on the part of large numbers of our people of the necessity for instituting more stringent conservation regulations to improve and conserve our resources, it is inevitable that developers will often find themselves on a collision course with the ecologists. In view of this, added consideration should be given by the buyer of a parcel of land as to whether necessary rezoning requests and building permits may be stalled or denied on environmental considerations. Federal agencies considering sites for housing, where loans are to be HUD insured or subsidized, will be extremely sensitive to objections raised regarding adverse ecological effects.

While our declining population rate may ease our environmental pressure over a long period, it is inevitable that our situation will get more critical before it improves. Once there seemed to always be new land beyond the horizon to replace that which was overused and abused, but those days are gone forever. Now plans must be devised which will permit development and economic growth to move in harmony with environmental quality. As we progress in this direction, the paramount problem to be solved is paying the bill and while government may bear some costs it is likely that the consumer will ultimately pick up most of the tab.

Emphasis has recently been added to environmental considerations as a result of population concentrations, intensified need for the production, and distribution of an unsatiable quantity of goods and a greater concern with the quality of life.

Like sex, which has also become a popular topic of the times, ecology, however, is not a new discovery.

Writing in the Journal of Forestry in 1933, Aldo Leopold said that, "man-made changes upon the face of the earth are largely the unpremeditated resultant of the impact between ecological and economic forces."

> If our system of land-use happens to be self-perpetuating we stay. If it happens to be self-destructive we move, like Abraham, to pastures new. Civilization is a state of mutual and interdependent cooperation between human animals, other animals, plants and soils, which may be disrupted at any moment by the failure of any one of them.

Ordering Topo Maps

Topo maps are available for most counties in the United States. These can be obtained from state geology departments, various dealers in most states, or from:

The U.S. Geological Survey
1200 South Eads Street
Arlington, Virginia 22202

The unit of survey is a quadrangle bounded by parallels of latitude and meridians of longitude. Quadrangles covering 7½ minutes of latitude and longitude are published at the scale of 1:24,000 (1 inch = 2,000 feet). Quadrangles covering 15 minutes of latitude and longitude are published at the scale of 1:62,500 (1 inch = approximately 1 mile). A few special maps are published at other scales.

Each quadrangle is designated by the name of a city, town, or prominent natural feature within it, and on the margins of the map are printed the names of adjoining published quadrangle maps. The maps are printed in three colors. The cultural features, such as roads, railroads, cities, and towns, as well as the lettering, are in black; the water features are in blue; and the features of relief such as hills, mountains, and valleys, are shown by brown contour lines.

A map should be ordered by name, series, and state in which it is located. In many instances, an area is covered by two maps which carry the same name, but are published at different scales. Where this occurs, it is especially important that the map order include the series designation, such as 7½-minute, 15-minute, or 1:250,000.

You may request an index, showing which maps are available for your state. The maps are inexpensive—usually 50 cents to 75 cents each.

9

CAVEAT EMPTOR

While many new regulations are being put into law for the protection of the buyer or consumer, I cannot overemphasize the importance of a thorough investigation before laying your hard-earned money on the line. "Caveat emptor," *Let the buyer beware*, should not be taken lightly.

Questions to Be Considered When Buying

There are so many different circumstances which may prevail when you are considering a purchase that a comprehensive, reliable check list is impossible. The following are some of the more important questions to be considered:

1. Are you getting a bargain? Some may consider buying land at its market value good enough. A successful speculator makes most of his purchases below prices being paid for comparable property.
2. Do you know the exact size and boundaries of the property? Even if you are buying by the "boundary" the exact acreage or square footage may be important to you when you resell or develop. On most tracts which I have bought, for some reason the owner always believes he has more land than stipulated in the deed. An accurate survey more often reveals he owns less land than stipulated in the deed. In addition to total area, the frontage on a street, or the length of a border on a lake or stream, may be important.

3. Will you be assessed for road, street and sidewalk improvements or utility installations?
4. Are you getting a good title? Rely on your attorney for this information.
5. Are you taking financing for granted? Whether the owner is carrying your note or you are financing through a bank or savings and loan association, *know,* don't guess at, the amount you can borrow and under what terms and conditions.
6. Is the soil stable? How much of the land is fill dirt? When was it filled? Was it compacted? Fill dirt which has not been stabalized may render the site unbuildable or cause an added expense for caissons or spread-footers.
7. What is the subsurface material? If the land is to be developed, removing rock may be prohibitive in costs and where multistory structures are contemplated, it is important to know the bearing capacity of the subsoil.
8. Is the property subject to flooding or other natural disasters?
9. What influence will the surrounding neighborhood have on future developments?
10. Is the property subject to unpleasant odors from nearby industries, stockyards, and so forth?
11. Is the property exposed to undue noise from factories, trains, trucks, buses, and so forth?
12. Are all utilities available? If some are not, how much would this detract from your projected highest and best use of the property? Also, mere knowledge of the existence of a sewer line or water line may not be sufficient. Size and capacity of sewer lines and capacity of the plant into which it empties may be important to you. Size and pressure of the water line is slways important and be critical where sprinkler systems are being considered.
13. Will the property enjoy benefits of neighborhood upgrading or has a decadance pattern been established in the area?
14. What is the street or road width bordering the property? Will widening likely occur in the forseeable future? How will it affect the value?
15. Is there a topo map of the property in existence? The amount of cuts and fills required to make a lot buildable affects its value.
16. What is the amount of annual property taxes? Are large increases forseen as a result of recent bond issues or proposed ones?
17. What is the distance to the nearest sizable shopping and employment centers?
18. Is the road or street well maintained?

19. Are you aware of all the restrictions and easements provided for in the title?
20. Is fire protection available?
21. How is the property zoned? Will there be opposition to changing the zoning to a higher classification?

Most of the above relate to the purchasing of unimproved property. Where improvements exist you need to satisfy yourself as to their conditions.

SURVEYING

In transferring property from one party to another it is essential that a positive and accurate identification be made of the parcel involved.

In the earlier days of the nation, identification and measurement of land for title purposes was generally handled by attorneys. This task is now normally preformed by licensed surveyors who may or may not be civil engineers but have established their competency with a state licensing board.

Proper Identification

Land being conveyed is most commonly identified in one of two manners:

1. *Lot and block number from recorded subdivision plot.* This consists of a map on file with the appropriate county official bearing the name or title of the subdivision; owner's name; surveyor's name and stamp; date of survey; and approval stamp of an appropriate county official(s).
2. *Metes and Bounds.* This type of description is used where there is no recorded subdivision plat. (Sometimes the buyer will insist on a metes and bounds description even with the presence of a recorded plat.)

Metes refer to measures and bounds refers to direction, and a narrative description is written using a definite, identifiable beginning point; corners of the parcel; length and direction of the sides of the property; and the amount of land contained in the parcel.

Another identification sometimes is the street and number of a house. This may be satisfactory for leasing but should not be relied upon in transferring title.

Large tracts in rural areas are sometimes described by monuments without exact measurements or directions. Monuments may be iron pins, stone pillars, fences or other artificial markers or may be natural markers, such as trees, stumps, streams, and so forth. As land becomes more valuable, these types of identification become less satisfactory.

The rectangular survey adopted by the Government in 1785, using meridians and base lines, applies to many states but not all.

Watch the Expenses

Professional services are expensive, but you can often reduce the costs by cooperating and assisting. Don't let a surveyor, his rodman, and two helpers spend time at $20 to $40 an hour looking for a marker which you can locate some Saturday afternoon.

Most surveyors mark points with small diameter iron pins with not more than six inches exposed above the ground. If these are in woodland or in a heavy growth of weeds and briers, the chances are you will be unable to locate some of them in a year or two. Calling the surveyor back to locate pins is expensive. Spend a few dollars for some iron pipe—cut into four foot lengths—and drive these in the ground two feet over the pins.

If there are old boundaries once marked by rail fences or Black Gum trees it may be necessary to get the adjacent property owner to concur in the new boundary.

Don't let the surveyor stop his entire crew and look for your neighbor. Find out when he will need a conference on the boundary and have the adjacent property owner(s) there.

If you are subdividing into lots or tracts to be sold at auction or privately, take advantage of the work performed by the survey crew in "hacking out" the lot lines. They will only do enough to get the crew and instruments through, but you may want a clear, well defined line when selling. Particularly in woodland the brush grows back quickly and two years from now you may not be able to follow the line hacked out by the surveying crew today. You can correct this by hiring day labor to go behind the crew and cut the line clean or use chemicals to spray the boundary lines in the early spring.

While most of these suggestions are somewhat elementary, following them may save you 25 per cent or more on your surveying costs.

How to Plot a Deed

Often when you are considering the purchase of a tract of land, you will find that the owner does not have a map of the property, only the metes and bounds description in the deed. In order to get a better idea of the shape of the property and to determine more accurately the number of acres, you need to make a map of the property—or plot the deed.

The only tools needed are a pencil and sheet of paper, an engineer's scale, a protractor—and the deed. Arbitrarily establish North on your paper, make a dot on your paper representing the beginning point as called for in the deed. Your first line will be the first call, which will give you distance and direction. Be as accurate as possible since a slight error on paper can create an error of many feet, and consequently you will not be able to close the plot.

You, of course, would not rely on your plot for a legal description, but it is an inexpensive way of getting a better knowledge of the tract than can be obtained by reading the narrative description.

Read "Computing Land Areas," in the chapter on Appraising, to learn how to compute the acreage included in the plot.

MAIL ORDER LAND BUYING

Earlier in this book I suggested to you that successful real estate speculators must be as concerned about *what not to do* as they are about what to do.

All across the nation, high pressure promoters are badgering citizens by magazines, newspapers, television, radio, telephone, and direct mail, to purchase lots, tracts, and acreage.

While there may be some exceptions to every rule, our advice on this type of real estate is *don't touch it with a ten-foot pole.*

Mrs. Roberts "Wins" a Lot

Some fifteen years ago, when I was in the real estate brokerage business, a dear friend of mine, Mrs. Roberts, came rushing into my office all smiles and exuberance.

"Guess what?" she asked, "I just won a lot in a nice new subdivision." "Well now, congratulations. Tell me all about it," I replied.

Mrs. Roberts told me she had attended a county fair and the developers of a subdivision were registering people for a drawing on a free lot, and to her surprise a few days later she received notice by mail that she had won.

She informed me that she had just mailed in her check for $173 to pay for having the title checked and other necessary legal and recording fees.

I asked if she had inspected her lot. She had not, but was going to look it over soon.

After Mrs. Roberts left, her "windfall" began to arouse my curiosity.

Very little research revealed that Mrs. Robert's lot was on a *paper* street, with no utilities, and no plans on the part of the developer to provide same, and guess what—every single person who registered for the drawing *won* a lot.

You see, the developers were working with $25 an acre land. Surveying and promotion were their largest expenses. Mrs. Roberts' lot was a quarter acre, and allowing for the "paper" streets they were subdividing each acre into more than three lots and grossing more than $500 per acre. Not a bad profit. Of course every winner did not fall for the deal and send their legal and title expense money in, but likely many thousands did.

It is unlikely that the legal authorities would permit such a hoax now, but relying on Barnum's theory, new gimmicks, which are technically legal or so marginally illegal as to invite few challenges, have sprung up to replace this one.

Misrepresented and Overpriced

It is true that with our growing population every year there is less land available per person—that no more can be found—it is the ultimate wealth—and with population pressures, its value must rise. In all likelihood you can, while blindfolded, stick a pin in a United States map, purchase the property you selected, and given enough time its value will rise over a long period of time. Some land is being promoted at five or ten times its present-day worth, however, and you cannot hope to live long enough to make a profit on this.

Shoreline, desert, wilderness, and mountain acreages are being subdivided by sharp operators and promoted with the paradise in the sun and retreat from the cares of the world pitch.

Many of those who have purchased lots unseen have discovered, only too late, they have overpaid—often many times—and the wonderful place for retirement or resale for profit is on a paper street without access, water, or utilities, and the nearest shopping facilities are miles away.

Often the names of sports celebrities and movie stars are used to entice the naive buyer. Before purchasing one of these lots for your children or grandchildren consider the fact that the probate costs may approximate or exceed the value of the lot. Some heirs have let these parcels revert to the development rather than finish paying for them when they got the facts.

Laws Tightened

Many states in which this type of promotion has been rampant in recent years are beginning to tighten their laws to give the consumer some protection.

California has chased many of the sharpies out of the state by enacting laws that require the developers to guarantee streets, water, utilities, and so forth. In all likelihood the fly-by-night promoters have found profitable refuge in other less regulated states.

The national Congress has also begun to take a hard look at flagrant abuses in connection with land sales. Congress passed a law in 1969 requiring each company promoting sales interstate to file reports with the Department of Housing and Urban Development. Disclosures relating to financing, availability of utilities, geographical information, and so forth are required to be furnished, and a copy of the report is required to be furnished the buyer.

13 Miles to Nearest Grocery

Recently, I responded to a developer advertising lots for sale in a western state. Amid his colorful brochures was a property report filed with the United States Department of Housing and Urban Development revealing the property was located approximately 50 miles to the nearest town of 12,000 population; the nearest grocery store, grade school, and service station were 13 miles away; the closest medical facilities and high school were 46 miles away. There was no public transportation and none contemplated. The plat had been on record since 1925 and only four of the nearly 3,000 lots had occupied homes. The lots were cheap–less than $500 each–the terms were good–small down payment and $10 a month with no interest charges. Fringe benefits included membership in an outdoor club, now in the planning stages and which promised to provide facts on relic hunting, fishing, hiking, climbing, and more. Lot sizes were about one sixth of an acre.

I have never personally inspected the area, because I could not conceive of anyone being interested in a small lot in an unimproved subdivision 13 miles from the nearest grocery store.

Obviously, however, many people are attracted by the magazine advertisements and follow-up promotional literature, since the developer reports 600 lots fully paid for and conveyed which would indicate that hundreds more are being paid for on installment contracts.

Many Will Buy on Easy Terms

Conclusions must be that there is a great desire on the part of a lot of people in this country to own a piece of land, and if it is cheap enough and the terms are easy, they will buy. Their chances for profit appear to me to be less than that of a ticket holder in the Irish Sweepstakes. While only a few may choose to occupy lots and tracts purchased in these remote subdivisions, perhaps others will reap their rewards in dreams of soft breezes, crimson sunsets, snow covered mountain peaks on the horizon—far away from the snarling traffic of polluted cities.

Although fast-buck subdividers are operating nationwide, the most prominent abuses have centered in Florida, California, west Texas, Arizona, New Mexico and Nevada. Many new developments are opening up in the east, particularly in the mountainous areas where cheap land can be acquired and where the property can be romanced by relating it to national parks, ski resorts, and so forth.

Also, there are many such developments springing up in the Carribean and Central America.

Florida—a Paradox

Florida is somewhat of a paradox in that it has offered some of the finest investment property in the country in the last decade, yet it has also been the largest base of operation for promoters who have peddled hundreds of millions of dollars of virtually worthless lots during the same period. Sadly, all of the promotion has not been done by small fly-by-night operators. Multi-million dollar listed corporations have had a heavy hand in many questionable developments.

The Florida land boom and bust of the 1920's was so highly publicized that many today are familiar with the history of these years, but few realize the 1920's was insignificant when compared to total parcels and total people duped during the 1960's.

Much land has been subdivided which is barely above sea level and remote from developed areas. Many parcels can be bought from original purchasers for a fraction of what they paid a few years ago.

Based on the current annual rate of building in some of these developments, it could conceivably require several hundred years to use all available lots.

Regardless of your age, you should have no fear that Florida or any other state is about to run out of land. The *Miami Herald* and other major newspapers have repeatedly critized the unscrupulous practices of fast-back promoters—but neither newspaper's criticism nor HUD disclosure requirements have been too effective in thwarting them.

A wholesale condemnation of recreational and retirement developments would be unfair. Some fulfill the promises they make and show you what you are purchasing. Unfortunately the legitimate operators seem to be outnumbered.

My advice to you as a speculator is not to consider property in one of these developments. Should you be unable to resist the fever, go look the property over and consult with local real estate agents.

Unscrupulous real estate promoters tend to rely on two basic ingredients:

1. Relatively cheap raw land—available to them in large tracts.
2. A locale which lends itself to glamorizing and romancing—where advertising can be related to tropical sun, ocean breezes, mountain skiing, hunting, fishing, and so forth.

HUD's Experience

HUD, which estimates an annual volume of five billion in undeveloped land sales, appears to be shifting from a stance of merely registering interstate sellers to an aggressive enforcement policy.

Officials at HUD say about 2,200 developers and 2,400 developments have been registered, but some estimate this represents only roughly one-third of the number that should be registered. Complaints from unhappy purchasers have been pouring into HUD offices at the rate of 200 a week, and a series of nationwide public hearings have been launched.

George K. Bernstein, HUD's Interstate Land Sales Administrator, said recently, "Although the land developments involved tend to be concentrated in the popular vacation and retirement areas of our country, no area is unique in being a target for promotions promising golden opportunities in second or retirement homesites and investment potentials all too often made by irresponsible operators whose only interest is in getting the biggest profit in the shortest possible time."

The Administration suggests that buyers contemplating purchase of land development property should, (1) get a property report and read it, (2) see the land, (3) exercise caution, and (4) learn to say, "NO."

Legislation may reduce the number of false claims and abuses, but many operators will find a way to stay legal while practicing deception.

Required disclosures, disclaimers, and rules and regulations, notwithstanding—so long as the buyers will buy—the developers will find a way to subdivide and sell.

Leave this to the dreamer. It is not the arena for the knowledgable speculator. CAVEAT EMPTOR!

10

ACQUISITION AND OWNERSHIP

Details are boring to many who like to buy, sell, and trade property but the successful speculator soon learns their importance. Many of these can and should be left up to your attorney, but some basic knowledge of the legal steps encountered in buying or selling is essential.

No attempt will be made here to cover every possible circumstance but I will review the major steps in a transaction by assuming you have decided to attempt to purchase a two-acre tract of land in your town which is listed for sale with a licensed broker. His authority to represent the owner is conveyed to him through *Listing.*

Listing (or Listing Contract)

Under this contract, which is signed by the seller(s), th property is described by metes and bounds or from a recorde plat; the selling price is specified; and the terms and condition under which the owner(s) is willing to sell are set forth. Listin contracts may be for any specified period of time. Ninety days t six months is somewhat normal and some contracts have a claus that automatically extends the time until the broker is notified b the seller. There is also usually a clause which stipulates that th broker is entitled to a commission if the seller conveys th property, after the listing has expired, to a party to whom th broker has "shown" the property during the period of the listin

Assume the asking price is $11,000, requiring 30 per cent be paid upon closing and the balance to be paid in equal installments of one, two and three years with the unpaid balance bearing 7 per cent interest.

You have contacted the broker and he has shown you the property. You decide $11,000 is more than you are willing to pay. The broker invites you to make an offer and you agree to pay $8,000. He informs you his client has already turned down a better offer and he cannot submit a figure this low. You reconsider and offer $9,500. The broker agrees to submit this offer to the owner. Depending upon the individual broker and the parties involved he may submit this offer by telephone, relay it in person, or have you write out the offer in your own words and sign it. Generally speaking, however, he will ask you to sign an *Offer to Purchase.*

Offer to Purchase

Through this instrument, addressed to the broker, you agree to pay the seller $9,500 for the property. The document should contain the following information:

1. Date.
2. Statement of your agreement to purchase.
3. Brief description of the property.
4. Consideration (in this case $9,500).
5. Terms and conditions.
6. Your signature.

The offer should be accompanied with earnest money to apply on the purchase price.

The broker may accept only your signature, or if you are married he may insist on both you and your wife signing and the signatures being witnessed.

Included at the end of the offer will be an acceptance statement to be dated and signed by the owner(s) and witnessed.

Since you will often be dealing directly with owners it would be well for you to have a supply of *offer to purchase* forms with owners acceptance clause included.

Instead of an *offer to purchase* agreement, the broker may use a form referred to as *earnest money receipt, binder agreement,* or *sales contract.* Regardless of the form used, the purpose is to obligate both buyer and seller under terms and conditions agreeable to both. These forms should be as simple and brief as possible, yet binding both buyer and seller to a contract into which each is desirous of entering.

You have now made an offer of $9,500. Obviously, the seller can reject it flatly or he might relay a counter-proposal through the broker. Let's assume, however, he accepts your offer. The broker returns the accepted offer to you having left a copy with the seller and kept one for himself.

In certain areas and under some circumstances it is customary to consider the above as temporary or preliminary agreements and follow up with a more formal contract of sale agreement. Usually this is not considered necessary unless the transactions are extremely large and/or complicated, so in your case the broker, through mutual consent, sets a date and hour for closing. Prior to the closing you want to be sure that you are receiving a good and marketable title, so you employ your attorney to make a *Title Search.*

Title Search

In performing this task, the attorney may trace the ownership back 50 years or more, or to a point in history beyond which he is convinced there is nothing of record adversely affecting the quality of the estate. Following the search he will prepare an *Abstract of Title.*

Abstract of Title

This consists of a brief history of title, summarizing the various links in the chain of title and setting forth liens, charges or encumbrances affecting the property. Utility, highway, and drainage easements, mineral rights, and so forth are identified in the abstract. In some areas it is customary for the seller to deliver the abstract and/or title insurance; in other areas it is the responsibility of the purchaser.

Should the examining attorney not be able to satisfy himself as to the exact description of the property he may insist on a *Survey.*

Survey

This is a process through which land is accurately measured and its dimensions and area ascertained. A licensed surveyor or engineer is employed for this purpose and should deliver to you a plat bearing the date of survey along with a certificate and a seal. Having searched the title and obtained an accurate survey, your attorney is now prepared to issue you a *Certificate of Title.*

Certificate of Title

If defects are found in the title, steps should be taken to remedy them. However, if they cannot be corrected with reasonable effort or are not considered damaging and you are willing to accept the title with the defects the attorney will list these as exceptions in his certificate. As a further precaution or to satisfy a lender you may desire to purchase *Title Insurance.*

Title Insurance

A flat fee is paid for the premium and the title to the policy is guaranteed. The policy insures for any undisclosed defects, subject to any exceptions set forth in the title policy.

Now that you are satisfied you are receiving a good title, you are ready to close. Actual closing may be performed by the broker through which you are purchasing the two acres or the broker may use a closing attorney. In either event you may have your own attorney present if you desire.

Normally taxes are pro-rated as of date of closing and although you will know from the abstract whether seller has paid his taxes, it is a good idea for the seller to bring his latest tax receipts to the closing.

The owner(s) may be present at the closing or he may have signed all necessary documents and left the closing up to his broker, in which event the transaction is being closed in *Escrow.*

Escrow

As applied to real estate, this term usually refers to delivering a deed to a third person (in this case the broker) to be held for owner or grantee until all conditions of the sale have been met and it is time for transfer to be made.

The most important document which you will receive at the closing is your *Deed.*

Deed

This is the instrument in writing through which you get title to your land (and technically tenements and hereditaments). This instrument must be signed, notorized, and delivered. We will assume that you are receiving the most common type of deed referred to as a warranty deed through which the seller covenants to protect you against any claimant. We also assume that, through the deed, you are receiving a *Fee Simple Title.*

Fee Simple Title

This term refers to complete ownership–free of all types of conditions and encumberances.

We will assume that your accepted offer of $9,500 was on the basis of $2,500 down payment and a note for one year bearing 8 per cent interest. The note will have been prepared by the broker and you and your spouse will sign same and, since the seller will want security on the note, the broker will likely have prepared a *Trust Deed.*

Trust Deed

This is an indenture in the nature of a mortgage, the execution of which conveys the property to a third person known as the trustee, who holds the trust deed for benefit of the seller or owner of the note. In some states a mortgage with only two parties, the buyer and the seller, is used rather than a "three party" deed of trust. The deed of trust should be witnessed and sealed (notorized).

Now that you have received your deed and executed a note and trust deed, the broker should give you a copy of the *Closing Statement.*

Closing Statement

In this event, your statement may be entitled "Buyer's Closing Statement," since in states or areas where brokers handle closings and make disbursements, it is customary to prepare both a buyer's and seller's closing statement. This may also be done where closing attorneys are used, or all the necessary information may be incorporated into one statement.

Each broker or attorney usually has his own particular method and form for closing statements.

Your buyer's statement for the two acres should list, as a record for possible future reference, the date of closing, place closing transpired, names of seller and buyer and spouses, and relate the names of those present at closing. This would be followed by the actual statement balancing out the funds and may look something like Figure 10-1.

	Debit Purchaser	Credit Purchaser
Purchase price	$9,500	
Earnest Money		$2,500
Note (secure by trust deed)		7,000
Attorney's fee		
Title Abstract	50	
Property taxes (pro-rated)	115	
Purchaser owes to close		165
Total	$9,665	$9,665

Figure 10-1

The seller's statement will be different from the above since it will include the broker's commission, attorney's fee for writing the deed and trust deed, revenue stamps, pro-rated taxes (which will likely be different amount from yours), and any funds withheld by the broker to pay off any debts against the property.

After the closing you will still have the expense of *Recording Your Deed.*

Recording Your Deed

If you use your attorney for closing he may handle this for you and list the charges in your closing statement, but in this instance the broker who closed has left the obligation for recording, and the charge for same, up to you.

Recording the deed should be done promptly since it is primarily for your protection. If you fail to record the owner could conceivably sell the property again, or could borrow money against it. Recording is done in the county of purchase with the clerk of the county, and serves as a notice to anyone that you now own this property. Years ago the clerk copied deeds being recorded in long hand. Most counties are now using a copying or photography process. Normally the clerk stamps the date and time on your deed, when you present it, along with the book and page where it is recorded.

The foregoing is merely an attempt to trace the necessary steps in a very simple real estate transaction. While a real estate speculator will benefit from some basic knowledge of the required legal steps, I advise you not to attempt to serve as your own attorney. Every transaction will be different and many much more complex from the legal standpoint than the one described.

Your challenge is to become a proficient speculator. If you accomplish this, you can afford a good lawyer.

Taking Title

I have seen closings held up for days because the purchaser could not make up his mind to whom he wanted the title conveyed.

Recently I sold a piece of property and the purchaser told me to convey the property to him and his wife. Before the deed was drawn he telephoned to say he only wanted his name on the deed. At the closing he changed his mind again and decided he wanted the property conveyed to a small, family-held corporation. My attorney changed the deed and we placed all the papers in escrow, with the purchaser's banker who had made him a loan commitment. In the course of drawing the trust deed the bank's attorney discovered the corporation was not qualified to do business since it had not recorded its charter with the county clerk. The transaction was ultimately closed but was very frustrating to me, my attorney, the purchaser's banker, and obviously to the purchaser himself.

I do not question the necessity of the purchaser giving ample consideration as to how he takes title, but particularly one who trades frequently in real estate should consult with an attorney in advance and receive advice as to the ownership or interest which best serves the purposes he is striving to achieve.

Some of the elections you have in taking title follow:

1. *Your own name.* Even though the property is in your name and you consider yourself the sole owner, most states recognize dower and curtsey rights, or community property rights, and your spouse will be required to join you in signing the deed when the property is conveyed. Dower is the life estate, given by law to a wife, in real property owned by her husband. On the death of the husband the wife is entitled to a life estate of one-third of the real property. Curtsey is the interest, recognized by law of a husband, in real property owned by the wife. This interest may be deeded by the wife during her lifetime or included in her will—either without the consent of her husband. If the right is existing at her death it entitles the husband to all net income for his lifetime.

   Many of the states have modified these rights or substituted other rights considered to be fairer to both parties.
2. *Tenancy by entirety.* When husband and wife take title together each becomes the owner of the entire property. Neither can convey or force partition during the lifetime of the other. When one dies the entire property belongs to the survivor. This form of ownership is nearly always used by a married couple in purchasing a home.
3. *Tenancy in common.* An undivided ownership in real estate by two or more persons. On death of one ownership, it passes to lawful heir or designee under the will.

4. *Joint Tenancy.* Undivided interest of two or more owners, whereby, on the death of one owner his share passes to the remaining owners (right of survivorship).
5. *Corporation.* This form of ownership is frequently used where the owner desires to avoid personal liability—although when using small corporations with limited capital, the owners will likely be required to guarantee personally any notes held by the original owner or a lending institution. The stock of a corporation is personalty, even though all assets may be real estate. For small transactions corporate ownership is often quite expensive, when costs of obtaining charter, keeping records, paying state franchise and excise taxes, and federal and state income taxes are considered. You may elect, however, to have your corporation taxed as a partnership by IRS. Advice from your accountant or attorney should be obtained when considering this type of ownership.
6. *Partnership.* Most states now have a "uniform partnership act," whereby the partnership is a legal entity and can own property. For all practical purposes, however, the owners are creating a relationship of joint tenancy or tenancy in common.
7. *Limited Partnerships and Syndicates.* See topics on tax shelters and syndication.
8. *Trusts.* Usually created for the benefit of surviving spouse and children—established by will or placed in effect during lifetime of owner. Most often it is used for income producing property, to be managed by a competent trustee, often a trust department of a local bank.

Good Records Are Essential

Most good real estate speculators are extroverts. They enjoy making a deal and dealing with people. They know how to buy right and sell at a profit, but they are bored with all the necessary nitty gritty details that go with the purchase and sale, and the in-between.

Proper records are essential. They need not be complicated but they should be complete, current, and accurate.

My records are kept by an experienced bookkeeper who uses a double entry system. Unless you are doing extensive trading, however, you should be able to handle the book work yourself using a single entry system. Keeping books on raw property is much less demanding than bookkeeping for improved property with monthly rental collections, repairs, and maintenance expenses.

The best system is not adequate if you do not get all the information down. *Pay everything by check.* Your tax accountant can recap your transactions from your check stubs. You will be ahead, however, to make your own entries. First of all, you can find out at a glance your total investment in your property in the event you receive an offer which you wish to consider, and secondly, you will save considerably on your accountant's fee if your records are organized so that he does not have to spend a lot of time in sorting and listing checks.

As soon as your transaction has been completed sit down and recap the sale while all the information is fresh in your mind. List the income received, less all your expenses including the cost of land, and you will have the profit (or loss) on the sale and ready to give to your accountant at the end of your taxable year.

Insuring Your Investment

Even though you may have never speculated in real estate the chances are good that you are fairly familiar with insurance as a home owner, or as a tenant owning your furniture, or as an automobile owner.

As an individual you cannot afford to assume your own risks and likely are not aware of the extent of your risks as a property owner. Consequently, the only sensible route is to select an agent in whom you have confidence and rely on his judgment or the combined advice of your agent and attorney.

There are two major types of companies:

1. Mutual companies.
2. Stock companies.

Mutual companies are organized on a non-profit basis and the interest is that they operate for the benefit of their members. Premiums are intended to cover losses of calculated risks and operating expenses. Surplus reverts to the policy holders in the form of pro-rata dividends or reduced premium costs.

Stock companies are organized for the purpose of returning a profit to the owners. The argument, as to whether a stock or mutual company is a better carrier for the individual, will probably never be settled. Some feel that while mutual companies operate more efficiently in the life insurance field, stock companies can better cope with the complex hazards of property insurance. To me the most important consideration is a good, reputable local agent or broker who, in all likelihood, will represent numerous reliable companies. Agents and brokers are in a good position to bargain and render service for you since the carriers rely upon them for business.

Another advantage of doing business with a local agent or broker is, if you should be traveling or sick when your premium comes due, you or your family need not panic in fear of cancellation. Like any other businessman, operating on a close margin of profit, your broker needs his money promptly and paying in this manner establishes your creditability.

Should an emergency force you to get behind in your payments, he will likely carry you for weeks or months and consult with you personally before considering cancellation.

When buying or selling improved property caution should be exercised to see that policies are promptly assigned or renewed after recording a new deed. Insurance does not necessarily protect property *per se,* but actually covers the insured against loss.

Since there is a professional lender involved in most real estate transactions, he will usually insist that the new owner is properly insured and that policy is assigned to him to protect his insured interest.

Most common coverages on improved property are fire and windstorm and public liability. Property owners need liability, not only to protect them against damages suffered by persons injured on their premises where the owner is actually liable under the law, but also against nuisance and forceful claims which are not justified but can cost the owner a lot of money defending his position in court.

There are dozens of other risks in addition to the above which you may want to consider insuring against. Some of these are:

1. Tornado
2. Hail
3. Explosion
4. Vandalism
5. Riot

6. Civil commotion
7. Water damage
8. Plate glass breakage
9. Sprinkler leakage damage
10. Leasehold loss
11. Business interruption
12. Rent loss

These and many others may be included in a package policy which your agent offers at nominal premiums.

The "Homeowner's" policy is a good example of a package policy whereby the insured is offered comprehensive protection at reasonable rates. This policy has received wide acceptance because many risks are covered under one flat rate policy resulting in a great savings over insuring under separate policies or riders.

Should you deal in improved property and employ persons for repair and maintenance, you should advise with your insurance agent whether or not you are required to carry workmen's compensation insurance.

Applying now to most all occupations, workmen's compensation insurance laws were an outgrowth of difficulties encountered by employees in recovering damages for injuries sustained in the cause of employment.

The provisions of this law, insofar as they relate to compensation or other benefits for personal injury or death covered by the policy, are made a part of the contract.

Initial premium is based on estimated payroll for the following year which is subject to audit near expiration of policy when upward or downward adjustments may be made in the premium.

Most of this brief discussion has concerned itself with improved property. I should also point out that you may have liability risks on vacant lots, tracts, and farmland which can be insured against at reasonable cost.

11

ANALYZING AND FORECASTING

Real estate is largely a "seat of the pants" game. Statistical data on which you can hope to base buy and sell decisions is sadly lacking. There are numerous indicators from which to base projections for a year or possibly two years in the future, but unlike traders in stocks, who may buy and sell with great frequency often expecting to hold their purchases no more than a few weeks or at most barely beyond six months, the real estate speculator must think in terms of two to four years–and longer.

While this situation may be enough to give many who survey the field cold feet, it can also serve as a blessing to the more courageous. For example, if you are trading in stocks, instead of real estate, and your broker or advisory service has just advised you that Spandex is about to receive patent rights on a new device for reducing automobile emissions, you will likely place an order. Your problem, however, is that a few thousand other clients of brokers across the country are getting the same information, and by the time your order reaches the floor the stock has already advanced five points from the previous day's closing. Your dilemma now is whether to keep buying as the stock advances? Will the price keep going up, or will your competitors in the market start profit taking and drive the price back down? Under any average set of circumstances your chances of making a killing are not great.

A similar situation can occur in real estate trading when a new shopping mall is announced for the west side of town. Hopefully, however, you will have one of two things working for you. As an alert speculator you will have known that negotiations were going on for the shopping center property and will have purchased some nearby land, or assuming you do not have this advantage you will have a better than average knowledge of available property on the west side. Who owns what? Who will sell? What are the chances for rezoning, and so forth? With this information your chances of making a good acquisition ahead of your competitors are good, even though the owners will demand a higher price than asked before the new mall was announced.

Since the real estate trader holds his average purchase longer than a stock speculator, he is concerned with long cycles as well as short fluctuations.

Cycles are sometimes categorized by economists as to their length as follows:

1. *Secular trends.* "Secular" relates to a long term of indefinite duration. The current rising price trend started as we began recovering from the depths of the depression of the 1930's. There have been numerous fluctuations during this period.
2. *Major business cycles.* Intermediate duration.
3. *Minor business cycles.* Shorter duration–perhaps two to four years.
4. *Seasonal variations.* Related to climate, tourist season, vacation periods, holidays and so forth.

The student of economics and conceivably the more sophisticated long-range investor of large sums may find it fascinating and/or profitable to pursue these theories at great depth and length; however, most speculators will leave these as a tool or toy of the professionals and address himself to more specific indicators.

Generally speaking a parcel of real estate will be affected by:

1. National factors
2. Local factors

Often local factors follow in the path of national factors, and this becomes more and more the case as the Government exerts greater influence through controlling interest rates, money supply, and so forth.

Federal Reserve System

Like many other segments of the nation's economy, real estate sales and development are influenced greatly by the action of the Federal Reserve System. Established by a congressional act in 1913, the country was divided into 12 districts with a federal reserve bank in each district. Technically, they are all owned by member or subscriber banks, but in practice they work closely and are influenced by the President and Treasury.

Interest rates have an effect on inflation and deflation and consequently the overall economy. The Federal Reserve has numerous devices for increasing and decreasing the supply of money, and this is an area where local conditions will follow in the path of national policy.

Interest rates will effect you as a speculator–first from the standpoint of borrowing on property you desire to buy and secondly, and perhaps more important, from the standpoint of the ability of the builder or developer, your potential customer, to borrow adequate amounts at favorable rates.

Employment Trends

Employment trends are great influencing factors. While most experts fail to agree with each other as to the perfect employment or unemployment rate, it is obvious that if the unemployment rate is excessively high, fewer people will have money to buy goods and services. There will be less demands for houses and apartments as families tend to *double-up* in periods of high unemployment.

Other Indicators

Other indicators include gross national products, average wages marriage rates, birth rates, population trends, retail sales, apartment vacancy rates, new house starts, construction costs, dee transfers, bankruptcies, and mortgage foreclosures.

For the average speculator and certainly the beginning speculator an analysis of the local market can be more significant tha ational figures. With a little effort you can become well informed n facts and trends in your local community.

Here are some of the things pertaining to your own community n which you need to be well informed:

1. Employment. Total numbers and percentages.
2. Wage scales.
3. Planned new developments such as shopping centers.
4. Prospects for new industries or expansion of existing ones.
5. Information on proposed new highways.
6. Population trends.
7. Financial condition of your local government. This is a good indicator as to future tax rates.
8. Apartment and single family housing vacancies.
9. Retail sales (trends).
10. Condition and attitude of local banks and savings and loans.
11. Real estate transfers.
12. Building permits.
13. Supply of property available. This becomes very important in communities "hemmed in" by natural barriers such as rivers, lakes, and mountains.

In the final analysis the price of a piece of property is termined by the highest price which someone is willing to pay r it, and this decision is made as a result of *supply and demand.*

nall Communities Less Affected by Patterns

You will note in the foregoing discussion of factors effecting e market there is considerable overlapping among national and cal factors. It should be pointed out that smaller communities not follow national patterns as rapidly as large communities.

A good example is the apartment business. Most new apartment ojects are initiated by developers or packagers. These people are ghly mobile. When the market becomes saturated in Dallas, they n move easily to Atlanta or Denver. They acquire land, supply chitectural drawings, and arrange financing and management. nstruction is most often done by local contractors.

Most of these developers are geared to larger projects—100 units d up—and operate in communities which can absorb these numbers. Consequently, the apartment market may be saturated in most of the major areas but with hundreds of small communities needing units which will go unsupplied unless produced by a local or nearby builder/developer.

I was told recently that 54 per cent of the housing in West Virginia was substandard, and while poverty had some influence on the situation, the primary reason was the lack of builders and developers in many of the smaller communities. It was pointed out there is a great demand for housing by people willing and able to buy, even in many communities with declining population, since so few new units have been produced in recent years.

Should you live in such an area we are not recommending you become oblivious to national statistics or forecasts, but it appears that most of the influences on your market will be local in nature. A national glut on the market in two bedroom apartments doesn't mean much in Madison, West Virginia if families there cannot find one available for rent.

Every Deal Unique

Even after learning all you can about your real estate market from every possible source, most of your decisions will be based on intuition and judgment. This business does not lend itself to standardization or easy answers. Every community, every piece of land, is unique. This increases the challenge and makes the opportunities for profit greater.

Stock market analysts at best come up with a lot of facts, theories, and projections. You can get reams of reports and some free advice—but no guarantees. Even the facts may tend to confuse you. Recently the Associated Press began including price earnings ratio in their daily market quotations. This is arrived at by dividing the closing price of a company's stock by its net income per share for the most recent 12 months.

If a company earns $4.00 per share and its stock sells for $96 its price earnings ratio is 24.

A quick review of New York Stock Exchange quotations disclosed P/E ratios varying from a lowly two to an astonomical 725. So, don't feel too badly at not having quarterly or daily reports on which to rely—they might just confuse you.

Growth and Inflation

With the national debt approaching the half-trillion dollar mark in 1973, interest for one year amounts to more than total cost of operating the federal government for the first 113 years. It wasn't until the war year of 1942 that cost of the federal government for one year exceeded 24 billion dollars—less than the cost of interest now.

Undoubtedly, future administrations, and for that matter future generations, will of necessity, wage a constant struggle to keep inflation at a "respectable" level.

Perhaps we take some comfort in the fact that while a few years ago most major industrial nations were keeping inflation under control better than we, the situation has now reversed and cost of living in such countries as Germany, Japan, France, the United Kingdom, Italy, Switzerland, and others is rising much faster than in the United States.

Among the nations encountering the greatest problems are many in South America where cost of living may rise from 20 per cent to 100 per cent and more in one year.

There is an old saying that the two things which cannot be escaped are "death and taxes." Now perhaps we should add inflation about which today's economists seldom speak of halting or reversing, but in terms of controlling. The consumer price index has risen every year with one exception since 1950. During these years the inflation rate has varied from less than 1 per cent to almost 8 per cent.

According to many prominent real estate agents and developers, the price of residential property in southern Florida has increased 75 per cent in the last five years.

An Atlanta newspaper recently reported that the price of land suitable for development has been rising about 20 per cent each year in the Atlanta area.

In terms of current dollars, per capita personal income rose from $1,501 in 1950 to $4,140 in 1971, and per capita disposable income rose from $1,364 (current dollars) in 1950 to $3,581 in 1971. Per capita personal income rose 80 per cent in the 1959-1970 period.

Personal savings rose from 13.1 billion dollars in 1950 to 60.5

billion dollars in 1971. Inflation and taxes had in 1972 reduced the purchasing power of the 1950 dollar by 38 cents "across the board" based on consumer prices according to the Department of Labor.

The real growth of the country is having a greater influence on real estate prices than inflation. In recent years the rate of real growth as measured by the gross national product (GNP) which is the total value at market prices of all goods and services produced by the nation's economy has been more than double the inflation rate.

An increasing population demanding an ever-increasing standard of living requires more and more land. The fact that new land cannot be created and the total amount must stay constant causes land prices to rise faster and higher in an expanding economy than prices of many other commodities, the output of which can be multiplied through more effecient methods of production.

Growing Economy

While inflation is reason enough for many people to invest in land, the big profits in recent years have been due to the pressure placed on available land by the growing economy. Even though the growth in the national economy may be only six per cent for a given year, the chain reaction may result in a parcel of real estate in a given section of your city doubling or tripling in a period of two or three years.

For example, if you have an industry in your city manufacturing air conditioning units distributed nationally, the increasing population demanding a higher standard of living (specifically in this instance more air conditioning units) may cause this firm to double its plant size and double its number of employees.

This will automatically cause a tremendous local increase in the demand for employee housing and land on which to build them. A portion of these people will want to rent apartment units which will cause developers to apply for higher density zoning which when granted will mean they can afford to pay more per acre of land.

The increased residential area generates a need for a new

neighborhood shopping center driving the price of commercial property still higher.

Emotional Influences

In addition to the factors of inflation and real growth, real estate prices may be emotionally influenced by these factors out of proportion to their real influences. For example, should the inflation rate rise in one year from 3 or 4 per cent to 8 or 9 per cent, it could cause a much greater increase in property prices due to a stampede on the part of buyers to hedge against further anticipated inflation. Somewhat offsetting this situation, of course, would be a reduction in "real" earnings leaving individuals with less money to invest in land.

THE GREAT DEPRESSION–CAN IT HAPPEN AGAIN?

Experience and common sense has taught us that there will be cycles in the economy–peaks and valleys–periods of tight money and high interest and of easier money and lower interest rates. Real estate transfers may fall off or increase for a given period due to fluctuations in the national economy or local influencing factors. These are reasons enough to cause us to budget reasonable capital reserves.

For those who raise the question of whether there will be another depression similar to the 1930's (and many do) the answer is that *no one knows, just as no one could forsee that one.* The answer which you must assume, however, if you are going to speculate is *NO*–1929 will not happen all over again. Perhaps it is a mixed blessing that your banker will not assume the positive *NO* answer along with you–particularly if he was doing business on Black Thursday, October 24, 1929, the date when the stock market fell apart, and the one used by most to mark the beginning of the panic of 1929 and the subsequent depression of the 1930's.

While there are no guarantees against a recurrence of this situation, there is now a more equitable distribution of income. Bank deposits are federally insured. The powers of the Federal Reserve System have been strengthened. Margin requirements are kept high; in fact, the speculator can be required to post the full price of the stock he buys. Unemployment and social security insurance are stabalizing factors. The Securities Exchange Commission attempts to police the stock market, and hopefully today's economists have a greater knowledge and understanding of underlying causes of depressions than the pre-1929 vintage.

Most national administrations now try to move quickly toward propping-up sectors of the economy. Politicians maintain constant vigil over unemployment figures. Next to wars, the health of the economy is the most critical of all questions of public policy.

Conditions Preceding the Depression

Most panics, no matter how complex their cause, have been associated with preceding excessive speculation of one kind or another. Periodic ececonomic crisis can be traced back to early civilization. Most people living in this country today are too young to remember the great depression of the 1930's. Fewer will recall a rather severe panic in 1920. A very few of our senior citizens may recall the "bad years" of 1903 and 1907. History records crises of varying degrees in 1897, 1873, 1857, and 1837. So, in one sense, 1929 was history repeating itself on a mammoth and dramatic scale.

The upward trend of stock prices which snowballed into the boom of the late 1920's began in the summer of 1921.

Florida Land Boom

Evidences of speculative fever were most apparent in the stock market but in the mid-twenties it broke out into an epidemic on Florida real estate.

With modes of transportation improving and incomes rising promoters were convincing speculators they should get a piece of the action before the mass migration from the cold North got into full swing.

Lots which sold originally for a few hundred dollars were selling for thousands of dollars and the price was going up with each new transaction. Prices of "inside" lots often ranged upward to $15 to

$20 thousand dollars and choice ocean front lots $50 to $100 thousand and up. More land was subdivided each day and even the scrub land and swamps commanded a hefty price. The cash problem was solved by using a finder deposit or small down payments of 10 per cent or less.

Most of the buyers had no thought of living on the land they purchased or even adding improvements for sale or lease. They had no idea as to the amount of land that was being offered or how many new citizens would be required to make use of it. They only knew the land was selling for more today than it cost yesterday and undoubtedly would command a greater price tomorrow. Traffic congestion became such a problem that railroads imposed a temporary embargo on the less essential freight.

Then in 1926 air started leaking from the bubble. The available land was far surpassing the number of new buyers. Two tropical storms in the fall that year, one killing 400 people and destroying millions of dollars worth of property, shook more bloom off the speculative rose. Promoters attempted to rise to the occasion through more eloquent persuasion but like the tropic winds, the tide of pessimism could no longer be held back, and by 1928 the Florida boom had collapsed.

This isolated happening may have had little or nothing to do with the depression of the 1930's but it's significant for the understanding of the prevailing mood of the 1920's. Interestingly enough, real estate prices, nation wide, were generally deflated during the 1920's.

Higher Stock Prices

While Florida was giving birth to a land boom—nurturing it for awhile—then losing the "child" in infancy—the stock market kept rolling along with higher prices and more shares traded.

Prices rose from the summer of 1921 to late spring of 1923; declining, rallying and declining again until mid 1924. Prices rose during the latter half of 1924 and continued through 1925. Early in 1926 the market dropped sharply then fluctuated throughout the year with year-end values about the same as the beginning.

Then in 1927 a steady increase began with only two months of that year failing to reflect an increase.

Adding fuel to the speculative fire was the reduction of the rediscount rate by the New York Federal Reserve Bank from 4 to 3.5 per cent. Some economists believe this easy money policy, enacted largely as an accomodation to friendly European countries, to have been a major cause of the boom getting out of hand.

Remember the market during this period was self-policed. No Securities and Exchange Commission regulated its activities. Stocks were traded on rumors, tips, and hearsay and the insiders made paper fortunes over night. New issues kept the presses busy and investment trusts, often started with a few hundred or few thousand dollars, sold shares to the public by the millions.

Following a setback near the end of 1927, the market gained in 1928 and receded again, and in the summer of that year moved on to new heights.

The market remained bullish throughout the summer of 1929 but the economy in general was showing signs of weakness and by fall the nation was in the early stages of a depression.

Worst Yet to Come

Economists continue to debate whether the failure of the stock market was the primary cause of the depression or a reflective mirror of a generally unhealthy economy—since the dull market struggled on until early September and the dramatic beginning of the end was held back until October 24th when nearly 13 million shares were dumped. But the worst was yet to come. On history's worst day in stock markets—October 29th—with the tape running hours behind, more than 16 million shares changed hands. The worst beating was, of course, taken by the weaker issues but the blue chips didn't escape with American Telephone and Telegraph dropping 34 points; Eastman Kodak dropping 41 points; and Aluminum Company of America dropping more than 50 points—to name only a few.

In the national election of that year, Herbert Hoover was elected in a landslide. Shortly before leaving office President Coolidge noted stocks were cheap at current prices and things were absolutely sound.

A leading economist had warned that fall of a depression if Al Smith should be elected with a Democratic Congress, but predicted prosperity for 1929 if Mr. Hoover and a Republican Congress were in power.

At about the same time Secretary of the Treasury, Andrew Mellon, reassured the nation "there is no cause for worry. The high tide of prosperity will continue."

President Hoover pointed out in his memoirs that he became concerned over the growing tide of speculation as early as 1925. It is unclear, however, what steps he inaugurated to convert this concern into a remedial action as Secretary of Commerce and during his early tenure as President.

The foregoing is not to place blame on any one individual, party, or group. It is presented here for two purposes, namely (1) to give you a sketchy backdrop of the condition and mood of the times, and (2) to point out that government leaders and experts could not clearly foresee the perils of the situation.

It is to emphasize to you as a speculator, based on past history, you cannot count on expert's from business or government having a great deal more clairvoyance toward these situations than you.

Perhaps another lesson which should be clear to us is that when stocks, real estate, or any other commodities are bought and sold with no thought toward their worth to an ultimate "user" the market becomes little more than a lottery.

Minor depressions, or periods of tight money and slowing down of the economy, occur frequently. Most authorities don't foresee a recurrence of the situation which prevailed in the 1930's—but they can't give you a guarantee.

In the 1930's unemployment was a national tragedy and the only commodity in short supply and in great demand was hard cash.

As compared to today, the Federal Government exercised few controls. It played an administrative role and to a great degree let everything seek its own level in the market place.

Today the government operates with a heavy hand and maintains a constant struggle to have near full employment and preserve the value of the dollar (check inflation).

As a real estate speculator you use your best judgment. If you are the more conservative type, maintain greater cash reserves. Your chances of making large profits will be less than the person who uses full leverage. Your chances of getting wiped out are also less. If you anticipate an imminent repeat of the 1930's you should not invest in property–invest in cash. Hopefully through our managed economy we can stave off booms and busts with our valleys and peaks not too severe and of short duration.

Other Land Booms

The student of economics may want to examine some land booms in this country's past, other than the Florida fracas of the 1920's, already discussed.

A boom occured during the 1914-1920 period and it was believed by some to have been triggered by unusually high wheat prices, coupled with the knowledge that there was no more free land in the country. Investors likely overlooked the tremendous ability of the American farmer to increase yields per acre through more efficient production.

The boom of 1854-1857 is usually related to the great westward expansion and high prices of grain on the world market in which the Crimean War (1854-1856) was an important factor.

Most historians credit 1832-1836 as a real estate boom period. During these years there was a great boom in Maine timberlands, caused by a fear that accessible timber was fast disappearing. During the same period there was great speculation in Western town lots and farmlands, based largely upon the Westward population expansion.

While each of the above were "big" in their day, they were puny by any comparison with the nation-wide boom of recent years, caused by economic growth, inflation, and the dwindling supply of good land.

12

BUYING AND SELLING FARM PROPERTY

Good farms offer many opportunities for sound, safe investments but are usually not excellent choices for a speculator, unless a use for the land other than farming is contemplated.

Where the land can be converted into a higher use, such as residential subdivision or industrial tracts, farm property is often an excellent investment.

Many speculators do trade in farmland (for farming purposes), and since we have discussed residential and industrial subdividing in other chapters we shall confine our discussion here to farmland for farmers.

Quick Profit on Farmland

The length of time required to hold farm property before turning for a satisfactory profit is a drawback to the speculator with the following exceptions:

1. You purchase a farm at a bargain price.
2. You recover a large per cent of your investment through sale of an existing natural resource such as timber, stone, or minerals.
3. You buy a run down farm and give it a face-lifting.

Knowledge of Farming Important

Your chances for success in dealing in farms will be enhanced if you fall into one of the two following categories:

1. You have a farm background and through experience have acquired an above the average knowledge of crops, livestock, soils, farm machinery, farm buildings, and the market value of farmland.
2. You are one of those individuals who, while not being farm reared, have a genuine fascination and love of farming and are willing to apply the time and effort required to learn those things which have become second nature to your country cousin who grew up on a farm.

Farms for Investment

If your interest is in investment as opposed to speculation, and you are motivated by a desire for a hedge against inflation, a farm with a minimum of improvements bought at a reasonable price is probably a good investment for you under most any set of circumstances. Some of the things which will help your investment work out include:

1. Low taxes. Farms usually enjoy a break on taxes through property classification which exists in some states or conservative assessments which prevail in many other areas.
2. Depreciation. Your land cannot be depreciated but your buildings, fences, brood stock, and so forth, can. If you are in a high income tax bracket your depreciation may more than offset your taxes. The purpose of depreciation is to allow you a reserve for replacement, but economic obsolescence may have already erased any true value of improvements—you may never plan to replace or repair them, yet they can be depreciated for tax purposes.
3. You may save considerable money by substituting farming for much more expensive forms of recreation. I know individuals who look forward to getting out to the farm every weekend and even on weekdays in the summer months, as soon as the office closes or factory shifts change. Some

people get as much enjoyment from this as their neighbors who head for the lake, river, or golf course. The farm hobbyist has no greens fees or docking costs, but likely charges mileage for at least a part of his trip which becomes a deductible tax item. Even if he only needs to see that the gates are closed, what tax expert can advise him that taking the wife and kids along for a walk in the woods, a leisurely horseback ride, or a few hours with a cane pole down at the creek, renders his trip for checking on the gates an ineligible deduction?

4. Free advice and counseling services. Federal, state, and local agencies offer greater assistance than you could anticipate in any other business or investment.

Agricultural Extension Service

Best known of the agencies that render free service to farmers is the Agricultural Extension Service. Nearly every county has one or more county agricultural agents whom you may consult in person, via phone or mail, or better still who will visit you on your farm, look your land over, discuss your special problems, and make recommendations–all without any cost to you.

County agricultural agents are professionals who hold a B.S. degree in Agriculture from a recognized college or university. Many hold advanced degrees and have years of experience.

Vocational Agricultural Departments

Many community high schools have vocational agricultural departments. Vo-Ag teachers have essentially the same training as county agricultural agents and render somewhat the same service on a limited basis, since much of their time is required for classroom teaching and supervising students' farm projects.

Soil Conservation Service

The Soil Conservation Service (SCS) is an agency of the U.S. Department of Agriculture and has local offices located throughout the United States. SCS is charged with the responsibility of developing and carrying out national soil and water conservation programs. This federal agency works through soil conservation districts, organized under state laws, and operated by local farm committees.

Technical advice, free of charge, is available on such matters as developing an overall farm plan; cover crops, farm lakes and ponds, septic systems, and many other things. SCS will assist you in developing a soils map indicating the most desirable uses for your various fields.

Agricultural Stabilization and Conservation Service

Still another U.S. Department of Agriculture Agency which renders assistance to farmers is the Agricultural Stabilization and Conservation Service (ASCS).

This agency administers farm price support programs enacted by Congress. It also administers crop allotment programs, the soils bank program, and so forth. County offices offer technical assistance on farm planning and shares in the costs of lime and fertilizer for pasture land.

No Shortage of Farmland

While it is true that land is the real wealth of the country and we cannot increase the supply, it is also true there is no indication of a shortage as related to our food production needs. This may appear unusual since each year we lose a lot of agricultural land to other uses, but improved farming techniques have more than offset the losses by increased production.

Urban growth has been absorbing farmland at the rate of about 750,000 acres annually. Roads and airports have taken another 130,000 and reservoirs take about 300,000 acres a year.

By the year 2000, according to an Agriculture Department study, the trend points to another billion acres, (about 3 per cent of the nations farmland) now used mostly for crops and live-stock—disappearing beneath population growth and demands.

According to the study published in the "Farm Index" b

Economic Research Service, about 57 per cent of the nation's land is used for agricultural purposes. Another one-third is in forests; cities use nearly 2 per cent; highways, railroads and airports use 1 per cent; with waste lands and other miscellaneous uses accounting for the remainder.

Before you get excited about capitalizing on a shortage for food purposes, remember federal farm programs have idled 50 million acres from the production of feed grains, wheat, cotton, and other crops to combat an over supply situation. Recent policies are returning some of this land to production.

Some Considerations Before Buying

If you are buying a farm either for investment or speculation and you do not have a farm background, get a friend to help you who knows farms and their value.

I have speculated in numerous farms—all with satisfactory results. (You do not make killings on farms bought as farms, and sold for farms.) Being farm reared and experienced as a county agricultural agent, vo-ag teacher and farm editor, I feel very comfortable when trading on farmland.

When buying a farm I do not enumerate things I observe or carry a list of important items because these have become second nature. You can bet, however, if I became interested in buying a stamp collection, something I know nothing about, I will get all of the expert advice available making a list of things for which to look, and take a friendly expert with me.

Some of the more important things to consider when evaluating a farm include:

1. Distance to nearest metropolitan area.
2. Roads. Conditions now and information on projected improvements.
3. Topography. Can you keep the land clean with machine labor. Labor for hand tools is virtually nonexistent.
4. Rock outcroppings. This can effect both cultivation and machine mowing.
5. Drainage. Watch out for conditions of severe erosion as well as marshy bottom land.
6. Soil types. The trained eye will be able to form a fairly

accurate opinion on the quality of the soil by observing farm crops, or timber stands. The uninitiated should consult the local county agricultural agent or soil conservation service. A soils map, which identifies soil types, field by field, may be in existence.

7. Timber. Your county agricultural agent can give you a ball park opinion but may be able to refer you to an area forester who is an expert and will advise you as to the amount and quality of timber, without charge.
8. Crop allotments. The amount of tobacco, corn, cotton, and so forth allocated to the farm can influence its value. Milk base is important for dairy farms.
9. Neighborhood. Is the neighborhood a desirable place to live either part time or full time? Is it accessible to churches, schools, and shopping? Is there a history of vandalism in the area?
10. Improvements. Observe the conditions of the house, barns, outbuildings, and fences. The conditions of the house may be important to you for one or more of several reasons:
    a. If you consider full- or part-time living in the house.
    b. If you contemplate using as a tenant house.
    c. Establishing its value for depreciation.
    d. As a factor influencing resale.

First, make a thorough examination of the foundation. If the house has a basement, start there. Look for dampness—an indication of surface water which may drain into the basement in extended wet periods or during flash floods. Also examine for dry rot. This is common expression synonomous with decay.

You can check the foundation from the basement, or if not a basement house, you will need to crawl under the house with a flashlight.

Most of the older farm houses are resting on pillars of brick or stone as contrasted to concrete footings, extending around the perimeter of the building, on modern construction. Are the joists, sills and plates solid? Have any of the pillars settled? The problems are expensive to correct. Next examine the roof as this is another major item of repair and/or maintenance.

Examine the conditions of the wiring, plumbing, heating system, fireplace, floors, bathrooms, and all other features. You may expect the room arrangement to be less than perfect. Stay away from major changes. Tearing out and relocating partitions can be expensive—since often your wiring and plumbing will be affected. Trim is hard to match in old houses. So, a little job that looks like it should cost $300 may wind up costing several times this amount.

As I stated earlier, if you are not farm reared or have not developed a love or fascination for a farm, your first and biggest mistake will be in buying one. Given one of these situations, however, a farm can be very rewarding and satisfying and a good long range investment.

FINANCING FARM PROPERTY

Fifty years ago one farmer produced enough for himself and three others. Today, he can feed himself and more than forty others.

The number of farms continue to decrease—size gets larger and capital outlay requirements have grown by leaps and bounds. An average of more than $45,000 capital is required for each farm worker—about twice the requirement for a worker in the manufacturing industry. While most conventional sources such as banks, savings and loans, and insurance companies are often used for farm financing, much of the capital for purchasing and operating farms is supplied by government agencies or government related lending cooperatives.

Most programs offered by these agencies are not tailored to meet the needs of a speculative buyer. You should be familiar with these, however, since your sale of farm property could depend on the ability of the buyer to obtain a loan through one of these agencies.

Farmers Home Administration

The most attractive loans to qualified buyers are offered by the Farmers Home Administration, an agency of the U.S. Department of Agriculture. Loans are made from funds advanced by private lenders and secured by the FmHA and from direct funds authorized by Congress.

The agency makes short-term improvement loans and loans to finance nonfarm enterprises on family farms, but your principal interest will be in long-term loans for purchasing farms. The loan amount may equal up to 100 per cent of appraised value not to exceed $100,000. The interest rate is 5 per cent per year on the unpaid principal. The maximum term is 40 years. This is subject to change.

According to FmHA, eligible applicants must meet the following requirements:

1. Have a farm background and experience or training needed to succeed in the proposed operation.
2. Possess the character, industry, and ability to carry out the proposed operation. When a loan that includes funds for nonfarm purposes is being considered, possess the ability necessary to carry out the proposed enterprise.
3. Manage and operate the farm and nonfarm enterprise.
4. Be unable to obtain sufficient credit elsewhere at reasonable rates and terms to finance the actual needs.
5. Be a citizen of the United States and of legal age.
6. After the loan is made, be a farm owner operating not larger than a family farm.
7. Be able to obtain operating capital including livestock and equipment.

A loan may not be made to an applicant who is already earning sufficient income to have a reasonable standard of living, even though he meets other eligibility requirements. A borrower may make large payments in years of high income to build up a reserve that may keep the loan in good standing during years of low income. Each borrower is expected to refinance the unpaid balance of the loan when able to obtain such refinancing at reasonable rates and terms from other lenders. Farm ownership borrowers are required to maintain their property and pay taxes and property insurance premiums when due.

Farm ownership loans are accompanied by technical advice to help borrowers make profitable use of their land and water, labor, capital, and other resources that will be available to them. The county supervisor furnishes advice on keeping accurate records of expenses and income and in budgeting and otherwise making wise use of income and credit. He also provides on-the-farm assistance with management problems during the first few years of the loan.

A farmer with nonfarm income may qualify if he is otherwise eligible.

Federal Land Bank

Another source of funds for farm purchases is the Federal Land Bank. While the interest rates are higher and loans are amortized over a shorter period than Farmers Home Administration loans, the agency is also less restrictive as to who can qualify. Current interest rate for Federal Land Bank loans is 7½ per cent and maximum term of loan is 25 years.

There is no maximum or minimum on amount of loan or size of farm. Part-time farmers, with only a few acres, can qualifty. For part-time farmers, farm income should be sufficient to meet necessary farm expenses and other income sources can be relied upon for living expenses and covering the loan payments. Federal Land Bank cooperatives serve all parts of the United States.

Production Credit Associations

For short-term operating and repair loans, many farmers rely on local Production Credit Associations (PCA's). These are cooperatives organized under the Farm Credit System. There are 450 PCA's with approximately a half million farmer-members throughout the United States. Farmers are currently borrowing about seven billion dollars a year through these cooperatives.

A farmer may obtain money to buy seed, feed, fertilizer and livestock. He can also finance a new truck, tractor, or other farm machinery. He may borrow to repair farm buildings or to modernize his farm home and according to a recent PCA circular, he may even finance his children's college education.

In each of the 12 Farm Credit Districts throughout the United States, there is a Federal Intermediate Credit Bank, a Federal Land Bank, and a Bank for Cooperatives. There is also a Central Bank for Cooperatives in Washington, D.C.

The Federal Intermediate Credit Banks make direct loans to local PCA's and discount farmer's notes for the local associations and other financial institutions. Each borrower from the Federal Land Bank or Production Credit Association is required to purchase stock in the Cooperative Farm Credit System in an amount equivalent to 5 per cent of the amount of the loan. The stock draws dividends when earned but they are not guaranteed. The stock may, however, be applied against the final payment of the loan.

FARM REAL ESTATE CHANGE IN VALUE PER ACRE, BY REGIONS, 1970-1972

Region	Percentage change during year ended November 1		
	1970	1971	1972
	Per cent	Per cent	Per cent
Northeast	9	9	9
Lake States	4	5	12
Corn Belt	2	4	12
Northern Plains	1	2	12
Appalachian	7	5	14
Southeast	8	8	16
Delta	5	6	9
Southern Plains	3	8	9
Mountain	4	4	9
Pacific	-2	6	4
48 States	3	5	10

Source: Economic Research Service, U.S. Department of Agriculture

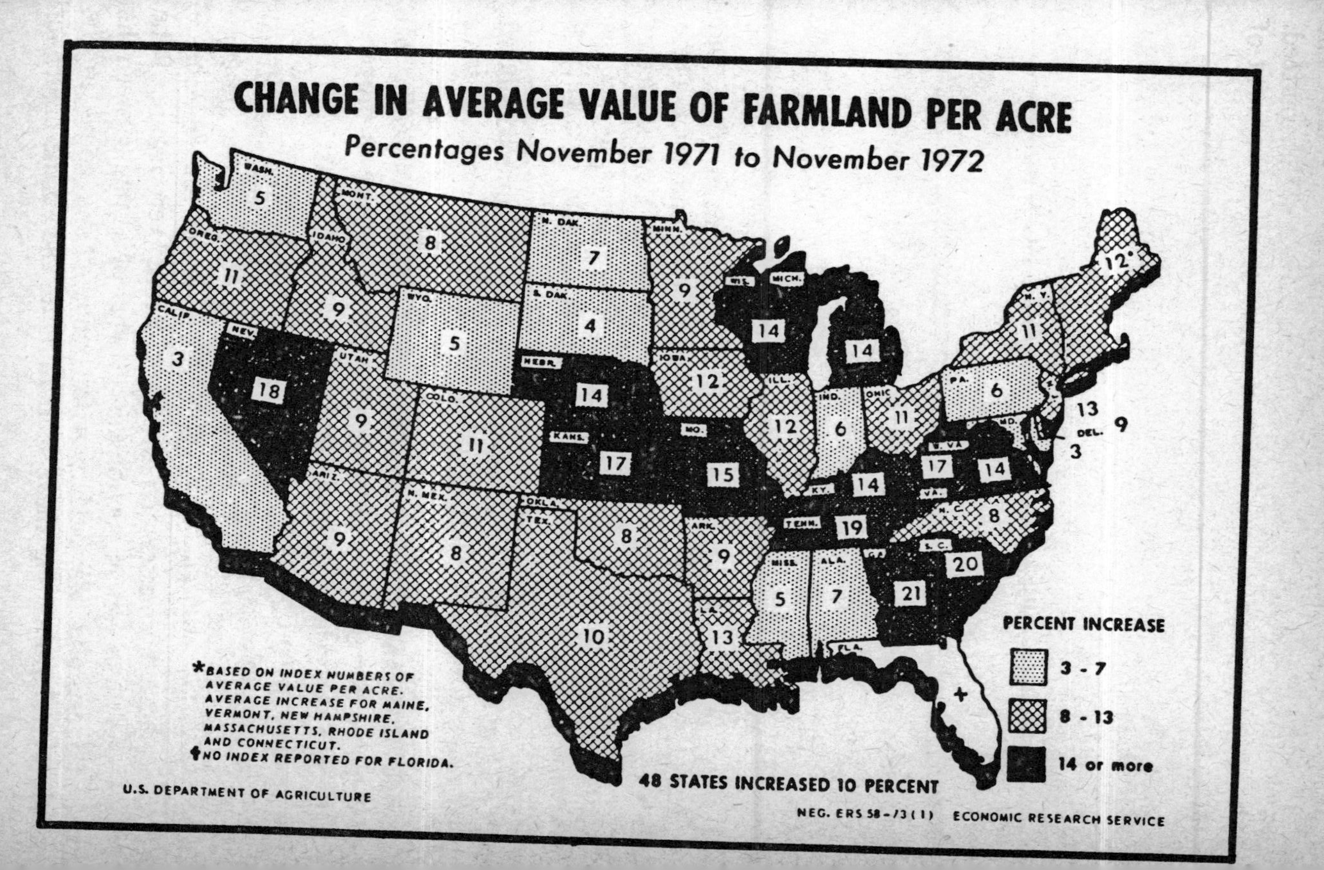
CHANGE IN AVERAGE VALUE OF FARMLAND PER ACRE
Percentages November 1971 to November 1972
WASH. 5
OREG. 11
CALIF. 3
NEV. 18
IDAHO 9
MONT. 8
WYO. 5
UTAH 9
ARIZ. 9
COLO. 11
N. MEX. 8
N. DAK. 7
S. DAK. 4
NEBR. 14
KANS. 17
OKLA. 8
TEX. 10
MINN. 9
IOWA 12
MO. 15
ARK. 9
LA. 13
WIS. 14
ILL. 12
MICH. 14
IND. 6
OHIO 11
KY. 14
TENN. 19
MISS. 5
ALA. 7
GA. 21
FLA. +
S. C. 20
N. C. 8
VA. 14
W. VA. 17
PA. 6
N. Y. 11
MD. 13
DEL. 9
3
12*
PERCENT INCREASE
3 - 7
8 - 13
14 or more
48 STATES INCREASED 10 PERCENT
*BASED ON INDEX NUMBERS OF AVERAGE VALUE PER ACRE. AVERAGE INCREASE FOR MAINE, VERMONT, NEW HAMPSHIRE, MASSACHUSETTS, RHODE ISLAND AND CONNECTICUT.
+NO INDEX REPORTED FOR FLORIDA.
U.S. DEPARTMENT OF AGRICULTURE
NEG. ERS 58-73(1)
ECONOMIC RESEARCH SERVICE

13

BUYING AND SELLING AT AUCTION

Real estate auctions are big in some areas and almost nonexistent in others.

Foreclosures and distress sales often conducted by an officer of the Court occur in almost every area from time to time, and sometimes offer golden opportunities for good purchases. These are usually sold for cash or on very short terms. Your source of information on these sales is your local newspaper, as the law usually requires two or more legal notices in a widely circulated publication.

Far more important to the speculator are auctions conducted by real estate agencies specializing in the auction business. In some areas auctions will account for 50 per cent or more of raw land sales. This can be an excellent method of buying or selling real estate or one of the worst depending upon the type of property and your knowledge of the business.

While not properly regulated in some states, most require real estate auctioneers to be licensed brokers or hold a special real estate auctioneer's license. Most firms are ethical, a few are close to the shady side. This same statement could, of course, be made about most businesses or professions. By the very nature of the business, however, an auction is somewhat of a game between the auctioneer and his bidders with bonus points going to the auctioneer for selling above market value, and to the bidder for buying a bargain.

Suitable Property for Auctions

At one time or another almost every type of property has been sold by auction. This method of selling is more successful, however, when many parcels are being offered, since you need wide interest to attract a crowd—and need a crowd to have a good auction.

When only one parcel is being sold, the greater number of uses to which the parcel can be put—the better—since this draws more people. Single family residences are among the hardest auction sales. Most houses are sold with very low down payment, and a loan to be amortized over 20 to 30 years. Often down payments, discounts, interest rates, and so forth become more important to the purchaser of a home than sales price. These matters are too complex to be handled in a limited time by an auctioneer who is not an expert in financing.

Best auctions are usually farms or large parcels of land subdivided into tracts and lots. Terms are normally 20 per cent to 33 1/3 per cent down and the balance in annual installments of three to five years with owner carrying the paper at bank interest rates or below.

The above situation usually brings out speculators in large numbers. They get the advantage of low down payments and enough time on the amortization to give a chance for resale for profit without a large investment, and little time and attention is needed to hold the property.

Farms usually sell well at auction, either as a whole or divided, when farm machinery, equipment, livestock, and household items are included in the sale. In this situation you have something for everybody and household items are excellent gimmicks to get the women out to a sale. Husbands who accompany their wives looking for antique milk cans, frequently go home the owners of one or more tracts or even a whole new farm.

I have described what I believe to be among the most desirable and least desirable types of auction property. There are many in-betweens, but the real test is usually whether you can attract a large number of interested buyers.

Real estate auctioneers use a chant that enables them to move along rapidly. Unlike tobacco auctioneers who are selling to professional buyers with their ears attuned to the chant, the good real estate auctioneer makes sure everyone can follow the bidding.

Types of Auctions

There are two basic types of real estate auctions:

1. Absolute auction.
2. Subject to confirmation.

With the first, the seller alleges he will convey the property to the bidder who offers the highest price. *Subject to confirmation* means the seller has the right to reject or confirm the sale, based upon whether he gets a satisfactory price.

Absolute auctions are by far the most common and most successful since they will command a better crowd and bidders will usually be more responsive if they know the seller means business.

How to Buy at Auction

Auction sales are usually advertised for several weeks. If you are interested in the property, spend some time looking it over before the day of the sale. If lots and tracts are to be offered, examine the size, shape, view, drainage, and other characteristics—parcel by parcel—and make notes on each one. Check carefully on available utilities, zoning and restrictions.

Consider joining with one or two friends on your first auction venture. This makes it more fun and you each get the benefit of exchanging opinions on values. One person may see something another overlooks. Never bid on impulse. Decide ahead of time what a parcel is worth to you, and stick to that price. Plats and descriptions of the property along with terms of the sale, are usually available from the auction company several days in advance of the sale.

When the Bidding Starts

The auctioneer or one of his co-workers will review terms and conditions prior to opening the sale. If there are numerous lots and tracts to be sold don't bid on the first two or three, unless you are absolutely sure you are buying at a good price. At many auctions the first two or three parcels are sold to prearranged buyers, in order to establish a satisfactory selling level, with the idea that subsequent bidders will gauge the value of the parcels on which they bid by the prices of other parcels previously sold.

If you are the first bidder on a parcel don't start it too high. Frequently the bids are actually started by the auctioneer, and the higher he can start the price, the more he will likely receive for the parcel. At other sales, bids are started by one or more persons working with the auction crew. The purpose of the starter is not so much to establish an artificially high price or to deceive the other bidders as it is to move the bidding along. Usually the bid is started at a realistic and acceptable level with the starter being an expert on property values in the area.

Often a well-attended sale will pick up enough momentum so the auctioneer will rely entirely upon the crowd for starting bids. It is the auctioneer's job to see that the sale does not slow down or lose its momentum and he will use all of his devices to prevent this from happening.

These aspects of an auction sale are offensive to some who classify starting bidders as shills and refuse to bid under these circumstances. In many areas, however, I have found this to be a common practice and accepted without prejudice by the buyers.

One practice occasionally employed but usually frowned upon by potential buyers is *bi-bidding*. This term refers to the practice of the owner employing one or more persons to *bid in* parcels on which the owner is not willing to accept the highest price offered by the legitimate bidders. Many speculators will walk away from an auction when they find this occurring—as they should. Most reliable auction companies will not conduct sales where this is prevalent.

With the best conducted auction sales, however, there is a constant cat and mouse game between the auctioneer and his crew, and you, the buyer. The goal of one team is to get the highest possible price while the goal of the other is to buy at the lowest dollar.

If you are new at buying property at auction sales may I suggest a little warm up period. Attend two or three as an observer to get the feel of it before plunging too heavily. Once you feel comfortable in pitting your wit and knowledge against the auctioneer, you may find this one of the most fascinating and profitable methods of buying real estate.

I have seen many sharp buyers make a 50 per cent profit on a purchase by reselling it before leaving the sale and in some instances to a person who was bidding against him on the parcel! I have also seen buyers get carried away by the fever of the sale and pay twice the market value for an item. Usually the best buys are made by those who have done their homework prior to the sale.

An auction sale may be your surest and fastest approach to cashing out a parcel of land. Many auction companies offer a complete service including boundary surveying, subdividing, advertising, furnishing ground crew and clerk for the sale, and even providing entertainment and food for the buyers.

While commissions charged by auction companies vary, 10 per cent is average.

14

DEPRECIATION AND TAX SHELTERS

Although you will need to rely heavily upon your accountant for advice on depreciation and tax shelters, it is extremely important that you acquaint yourself with some basic knowledge of the subjects.

DEPRECIATION

Depreciation is usually defined as *a loss of value for any cause.* A farmer buys a tractor for $6,000. At the end of six years it is worn out. If he has had to pay taxes on all the dollars he has earned with the tractor during this period he may not have the money to replace it. The government recognizes this problem and permits him to set aside each year one-sixth of the cost of the tractor, or $1,000 on which he does not have to pay taxes.

Economic Obsolescence

Depreciation, however, is not confined to *using up* or *wearing out*. Constant change is a way of life in our society. We are always looking for an easier, better way, and whether better or not, our ideas and tastes change. For these and other reasons a building or an item of personal property may become obsolete long before it is worn out.

A calculator bought by an insurance agency three years ago anc designed by the manufacturer to give service for 10 to 20 or ever 30 years is now in the storage room covered with dust. Is it worn out? Absolutely not, practically as good as new. It has beer replaced by a new electronic model which is quieter, faster, anc easier to operate.

In the downtown area of most any small town there is a multistory hotel. The spacious lobby, marble floors, and ornate woodwork were at one time the pride of the owners and the community. Materials and workmanship were of the highes quality. The building is solid as a rock (we can no longer use "sound as a dollar"). To duplicate it today would cost a fortune

It suffers from lack of parking, no central air conditioning manual elevators, and small, high-ceiling rooms. Tourists anc commercial travelers are stopping at the new Holiday Inn. The building is a victim of economic obsolescence.

Most properties, however, have enjoyed a happier fate.

The chances are that well-located and well-kept single famil residences, apartment buildings, and in some instances offices an commercial buildings are worth more now than their value 2 years ago.

If you had owned any of these properties you would have bee permitted to take a depreciation every year on your income ta (or throughout the useful life as determined by IRS). This is on of the big attractions of real estate investing.

Calculating Depreciation

There are three major methods of depreciation recognized b the IRS:

1. Straight Line.
2. Declining Balance.
3. Sum-of-the-digits.

Straight Line Method

Using the straight line method, the value of the building i divided by the expected useful life of the building to get the rat of depreciation.

Example: A $100,000 building has a remaining economic life of 40 years.

$\frac{\$100,000}{40}$ = $2,500 depreciation a year or a rate of 5 per cent annually.

Declining Balance

Using the declining balance, or fast write-off approach, you may double the straight line rate on government rent subsidized dwelling structures and in some instances, explained later in the topic on "Tax Shelters," on other projects. By this method the above building could be written-off at the rate of 10 per cent per annum instead of 5 per cent. This would be referred to as the 200 per cent declining balance method.

A declining balance of 150 per cent is the maximum allowed on most buildings. For these we use one and one-half times the straight line rate. In this instance the rate of depreciation on a $100,000 building would be 7½ per cent or $7,500 the first year.

You may be able to further accelerate the depreciaton by itemizing the components of the building. For example, the useful life of the air conditioning system may only be 12 years, while the foundation may be expected to have an economic life of 50 years.

Sum-of-the-Digits

The other fast write-off method is referred to as sum-of-the-digits.

Example: A $100,000 building with a remaining economic life of 10 years.

1st year: $\frac{10}{55}$ x $100,000 = $18,180
(1+2+3+4+5+6+7+8+9+10 = 55)

2nd year: $\frac{9}{55}$ x $100,000=$16,362, etc.

The fast write-off method is designed to give high deductions in the early years of ownership and reduced deductions in the later years.

After deductions diminish to the point they are no longer useful as write-offs to the taxpayer, the property may be sold and the advantage of long term capital gains taken. The seller must be careful, however, not to sell too soon or he may be penalized by IRS.

TAX SHELTERS

Under present tax laws, the significance of depreciation has increased to the point where tax leveraging has become the prime motivating factor in many real estate transactions. A doctor making $100,000 a year needs additional taxable income like he needs a left-handed stethoscope. At the same time a $50,000 tax loss could be the greatest thing since Medicare.

Much of the action in improved real estate has been generated in recent years by persons in high income brackets seeking to reduce or defer annual income tax liability. Tax laws making this possible are hailed by some as a necessary catalyst in the production of housing to meet the nation's shelter requirements, by others as loopholes benefiting the rich at the expense of the poor.

Using rapid depreciation methods permitted by the IRS, losses are established when the operating costs, interest, and depreciation exceed the rental income. These losses are recognized by IRS even when the value of the property may be increasing due to inflation, higher replacement cost, and so forth. The losses may occur even though the owners are receiving a cash flow return.

Such investments are usually referred to as tax shelters. The benefits may be derived through the effect of reducing one's net investment in a speculative venture but more commonly the benefits occur through the *sheltering* of other income of the investor. These are widely used by doctors, lawyers, and other professional people in a high income bracket.

Benefits Multiplied

The benefits derived from such investments are multiplied through *leverage.* Using our doctor friend as an example again, let's say he has three children in college, big house payments, and a wife who likes to be kept in a style which she never could afford as a third-grade teacher. All the neighbors whom he overcharges believe he is getting rich but his banker, whom he calls on in early April every year for a tax loan, knows better.

He already has several deductions including interest on his house mortgage, interest at the bank, expense of his office and automobile, but he is still having a terrific tax obligation. He doesn't have a half million dollars to invest in an apartment house or a neighborhood shopping center, but doctors are good credit risks. He can borrow $50,000 as a personal loan. He can take the $50,000 and use it as equity or down payment on a half-million dollar building and hire good management for the property. He should get enough tax benefits during the first two years–three at the most to repay his $50,000–then he has a free ride for several years. Obviously, he will use the fast write-off approach, and depending on the type of project and how his accountant sets up his books, he will need to sell this property in 10 to 15 years and buy something else.

If he doesn't want to bother with actually owning property he can accomplish the same thing by buying percentage shares from a syndicator (see chapter on Syndication) but he will be paying off more middle men and his $50,000 will not buy as much.

Federal Housing Administration projects for the low or moderate income requires approximately 10 per cent equity on the part of the owners. Let's suppose a developer puts together a project costing one million dollars in addition to the price of the land. He keeps 10 per cent ownership and becomes the general (managing) partner and sells 10 per cent interest to nine other people for $11,000 each–representing 10 per cent of the cost of the project–plus 10 per cent of the land cost, assumed to be $100,000. For an $11,000 investment, each investor would receive the benefit of the depreciation on $100,000.

To have accomplished this, it is likely a limited partnership form of ownership would have been used since it protects the investors from the chance of suffering losses in excess of his original contribution should the project get into financial distress due to low occupancy rates, inefficient management, and so forth.

The above illustration is somewhat oversimplified. In an actual transaction the developer or packager would have demanded more than $11,000 from each investor–since this would have been his principal vehicle for profits and the investor could afford to pay the developer a profit and still have a favorable buy. The amount which the investor can afford to pay is closely related to the amount of income to be sheltered, or since these investments are worth more to individuals in high tax brackets, they are normally priced beyond the reach of low tax bracket investors.

Most Favorable Shelters

Among the more favorable tax shelters are those created through structuring low and moderate income housing programs under the provisions of Section 236 and 221 (d)(3) and other programs of the National Housing Act. Advantages are gained through acclerated depreciation methods, liberal depreciation recapture rules, and the postponement of taxation on the sale of a project. There is great leverage advantages through 90 per cent loan and a 40-year mortgage provisions. Depreciation recapture rules, on the above projects, permit excess depreciation (over straight-line) to be taxed at capital gains rates, after 120 months of operations. Government subsidized programs may be changed or discontinued and anyone seeking tax shelters should stay current on the status of the various programs.

Taxes may be further postponed by selling one of the above projects and reinvesting in a like property.

The fast write-off, double declining balance, or sum-of-the-years-digits methods may be used to depreciate any new residential property. New non-government subsidized residential property must be held 200 months to permit the excess of accelerated over straight line depreciation to be taxed entirely at capital gains rates when the property is sold.

Owners of nonresidential property must recapture all of the excess accelerated depreciation as ordinary income when they sell their properties.

Current IRS Guidelines

As this is written, I am advised by my certified public accountant that the following application is being followed:

1. Low and moderate income government housing–double declining balance (DDB) and other special considerations.
2. New residential rental property–double declining balance.
3. Used residential rental property–one and one-half straight line.
4. New commercial property–one and one-half straight line.
5. Used commercial–straight line.
6. Single family residence–straight line.

A partner and I own a 75 unit FHA 236 apartment project on which construction was completed in 1970. By using the 200 per cent declining balance method and breaking out the building components in order to receive the fastest possible depreciation, we each initially received more than $40,000 a year in tax shelter benefits. This amount will be reduced each year as the depreciation benefits are exhausted.

IRS rules affecting depreciation and regulations affecting recapture on tax shelters are subject to change. These matters can be most confusing to laymen and with the frequent changes and the gray areas, which sometimes can only be resolved by court cases–are often even perplexing to competent accountants.

Like numerous other topics, Depreciation and Tax Shelters are discussed here to help you evaluate the worth of unimproved property to a prospective purchaser who contemplates improvements and is primarily motivated by tax sheltering advantages.

Should you need information on depreciaton and tax sheltering on improved property you contemplate buying or building, consult with a capable accountant. The foregoing should arm you with enough information to converse intelligently with a purchaser of land for these purposes. While they say a little learning is a dangerous thing, I have also found it helpful in analyzing the position of my prospects.

Depreciation Schedule

The 1971 depreciation schedule (Figure 14-1) was for a 75 unit FHA 236 apartment project owned by the writer and a partner on which construction was completed in 1970.

GARDEN VALE APARTMENTS

	Project Cost by Line Items	Straight Line Depreciation
Concrete	$ 37,159	$ 743
Masonry	65,544	1,311
Metals	8,597	430
Rough Carpentry	103,839	2,077
Finish Carpentry	54,584	3,639
Waterproofing	1,605	32
Insulation	11,672	233
Roofing	15,156	758
Sheet Metal	1,832	37
Doors	25,717	1,714
Windows	10,247	683
Drywall	45,591	1,824
Tile Work	5,297	530
Resilient Flooring	18,720	1,872
Painting and Decorating	22,481	7,494
Specialties	4,138	828
Special Equipment	1,343	268
Cabinets	21,987	2,199
Appliances	21,672	2,167
Plumbing and Hot Water Fixtures	46,952	3,130
Other	21,915	877
Air Conditioning	52,976	3,532
Electrical–Fixtures	6,429	429
Wires	40,163	1,607
Earth Work	20,089	402
Site Utilities	8,130	163
Roads and Walks	23,791	4,758
Site Improvements	2,224	44
Lawns and Planting	14,719	981
Totals	$714,569	$44,762

FIGURE 14-1

DEPRECIATION SCHEDULE

Depreciation Percent/Years (DDB)	First Year Depreciation (4 mos.)	Second Year Depreciation
4/50	$ 495	$ 1,467
4/50	874	2,587
10/20	287	831
4/50	1,385	4,098
13 1/3/15	2,426	6,953
4/50	21	63
4/50	156	461
10/20	505	1,465
4/50	24	72
13 1/3/15	1,143	3,276
13 1/3/15	455	1,305
8/25	1,216	3,550
20/10	353	988
20/10	1,248	3,494
66 2/3/3	4,996	11,657
40/5	552	1,434
40/5	179	466
20/10	1,466	4,104
20/10	1,445	4,045
13 1/3/15	2,086	5,981
8/25	584	1,707
13 1/3/15	2,354	6,748
13 1/3/15	286	819
8/25	1,071	3,127
4/50	268	793
4/50	108	321
40/5	3,172	8,248
4/50	30	88
13 1/3/15	654	1,875
	$29,839	$82,023

15

SYNDICATING REAL ESTATE

There are numerous ways to invest in real estate other than the outright purchase of property. Syndication is one. The term has numerous applications but let us first briefly examine public syndication.

Public Syndication

A syndicator is basically a middle man. He buys property from builders, developers, and other owners of real estate, divides the property into limited partnership shares and sells these shares to investors.

Syndication may be divided into specific property offerings and blind pool offerings. Using a specific property offering, the syndicator enters into contract with the developer and/or builder and prior to the loan closing he advances the money to close the transaction.

In a blind pool offering, the syndicator raises the money first without a specific property in mind. He then goes to the developer with cash in hand for the purchase.

The builder/developer may become the general partner retaining a 5 per cent interest, or the syndicator may assume this role. The general partner assumes the risks and management responsibilities.

The syndicator then divides the property into small units ($5,000 multiples) and sells the units, often through securities brokers. He registers the property through the Securities Exchange Commission or appropriate state regulatory agency.

The limited partnership form of ownership is used because investors do not want to put in $5,000 and be called upon later to ante up again, nor do they want to be sued when someone is injured on the premises.

Investors are normally persons in a high income bracket since depreciation is very valuable if you are in the 35 per cent to 50 per cent income tax bracket.

Syndicators also look for 7 to 10 per cent cash flow. The proper combination of cash flow, tax write-offs, equity build-up, and capital appreciation are the necessary ingredients of a good syndication project.

Many types of property are syndicated; however, most syndicators specialize in apartments with emphasis on subsidized government projects where IRS permits the use of the 200 per cent declining balance depreciation method.

Some builder/developers handle their own syndication without employing the services of a middle man. Care must be exercised in doing this not to run afoul of SEC or state regulatory regulations.

As in any other venture, careful examination should be made before investing your money in a real estate syndicate. You are more likely to lose your equity in a yet to be built project, than an existing one. Rents may be overestimated but far more dangerous is construction costs and syndication usually does not raise enough money to handle emergency situations.

These are two major kinds of risks:

1. The project may fail to return projected income and hence will be less valuable than you thought.
2. Through vacancies or reduced rent brought on by competition, the income may fall off to where syndicate can no longer meet management, maintenance, taxes, and mortgages.

Real Estate Investment Trusts

A Federal Court decision in 1936 hit hard at Real Estate Investment Trusts with a ruling that they must be classified as corporations and were liable for corporate taxes before paying dividends. Prior to this time these trusts which originated in

Boston, Massachusetts in the 19th century, had spread successfully across the country.

It was 1960 before Congress was persuaded to amend the tax laws, again permitting investors in Real Estate Investment Trusts to avoid double taxation. The device even then was not returned to its pre-1936 status since numerous requirements must be met before it could qualify for corporate tax exemptions.

The new law stipulated that 75 per cent of the REIT's gross income must come from investments related to real estate and not more than 25 per cent of total assets could be in nonreal estate investments. It specified a minimum of 100 share holders and not more than 50 per cent of the stock could be held by fewer than five persons. It also required at least 90 per cent of the annual net income be paid to investors in order to qualify for corporate income tax exemption.

A further restriction stipulates capital gain on securities held less than six months and on property held less than four years must constitute less than 30 per cent of the gross income–limits the trusts appeal to a speculator.

Also, the fact that the trust must disperse 90 per cent of its income to its investors annually precludes a healthy environment for growth.

Private Syndication

Often a speculator will come across a piece of property appearing to offer excellent profit potential but the amount of capital required and/or the risk assumed is too great.

Given this situation, he can pass up the property and seek something within his means or he can associate himself with friends and acquaintances who will share the cost and the risk–the profits or the losses.

Such a group is often referred to as a syndicate. Sometimes it is called a joint venture. It most often operates as a partnership to avoid the double taxation effect of a corporation. If an individual enters into a partnership arrangement, it should be with persons he knows and trusts, and he should keep himself fully informed on all transactions, otherwise either dishonesty or bad judgment on the part of the active partner could result in financial disaster.

Two important benefits to be gained from entering into a joint venture are the increased value of the project resulting from the complementary interests of the money partner(s) and the work partner, and the ability to expand the development operation and generate greater economic benefits.

Benefits to money partners:

1. Potential return is greater from active involvement than from passive position such as mortgagee.
2. Investors usually do not have time and skills required.

Benefits to developer:

1. Source of money through all types of money markets.
2. Provides holding power and flexibility to respond to changes in the market.
3. Money partner may have valuable contacts.

Major determination of money partner is how much risk he will take. Structuring partnership is very important. The structure should reflect conclusions about risk taking and economic desires.

If the syndicate is contemplated as a long range structure, and one that may invest in numerous properties, it may be well to consider forming a corporation to limit the risk to the individuals.

Naturally, you will rely on the advice of your attorney or auditor in this matter, but there are at least two alternate approaches whereby you may in effect be able to eat your cake and have it too. You may designate your corporation a Sub Chapter S Corporation—whereby you will have the normal corporate advantages of limiting your risk but you will be taxed as an individual on any profits.

You may also operate your syndicate on a limited partnership basis with one or more members functioning as the general partner and assuming the management responsibilities and liabilities.

There are many disadvantages in syndicates but the one major advantage of being able to handle larger deals may offset all the others. As a general rule, the larger deals will be proportionately more profitable than the smaller ones, because there is far less competition.

For example, almost anyone who trades in real estate in your area is potential competition on a $5,000 residential lot or a $10,000 commercial lot, but few will have the cash it takes to swing deals of $100,000 to $200,000 transactions and many of those who do will not want to tie this much capital up in one deal.

Many of the problems in private syndicates center around putting a compatible group together, then once you have it together, keeping it compatible. If decisions are to be made jointly or by the majority, the group should be limited to not more than five participants–and even with this number your first problem will be in getting a quorum when a decision is needed. Your second problem will likely be getting the individuals to agree.

Where there are more than two or three partners, the best solution is often to designate an active partner to handle all transactions, with the other partners functioning as investors. The active partner must be both knowledgeable and trustworthy and he must be well-compensated for his efforts. The syndicate has often been abused by promoters who find a deal, solicit numerous investors, then take a big cut for finder's fee. In some instances these people have taken anywhere from one-sixth to one-third ownership as their cut for assuming legal liability, then quickly reselling the property, pocketing their share of the selling price and leaving the investors unhappy.

The New Breed–Real Estate Packagers

While developers, promoters, and packagers have been around for a long time, they have taken on new dimensions with the advent of turnkey public housing and subsidized HUD programs.

The terms as applied to real estate defy definition. The term *developer*, preferred by many real estate operators, may be applied to an individual or group who originates an idea and carries it all the way through planning, acquiring real estate, financing, and building, or it may be limited to one or more of these phases.

Some facetiously say that a developer is a promoter with money.

Promoters or *packagers* are terms usually applied to those who are skilled in putting a deal together to the point where it needs strong financing and construction expertise.

As in most businesses, real estate has its share of unethical fast buck operators, but promoters or packagers may render a very necessary service. Many of the newer government housing programs are so complex the average investor and most building contractors do not have the know-how or the time to learn how to put them together.

Many non-government programs fall into the same category with shopping centers perhaps being the prime example. Many apartment complexes including cooperatives and condominiums are conceived by packagers who option or purchase land, make a feasibility study, prepare a preliminary lay-out, then sell to a builder/developer.

16

APPRAISING FOR SPECULATION

An *appraisal* is an estimate of the value of a parcel of real property.

If you are to be a successful real estate speculator, you must become capable of doing your own appraising. The competence of your judgment of values will determine more than anything else your success or failure in this business.

I have speculated in real estate most of my adult life and have yet to feel the need of a professional appraiser when buying or selling vacant land—other than where an appraiser was required to satisfy a second or third party.

You cannot, however, deal in real estate and completely by-pass professional appraisers since you will be borrowing money from banks, savings and loans, and insurance companies—all of which will use professional appraisers. At least they will use their own designated appraisers but there will be times when you may question their "professional ability."

There are many appraisers who are truly professional and these are essential to the real estate business. Thousands of professional appraisers are employed or retained by government agencies in connection with acquisition of right-of-ways and whenever property is being acquired or disposed of by governmental agencies. Their services are also required by many publicly held corporations when buying or disposing of property and in the division of estates in both friendly and disputed situations. HUD appraisers place a value on property where loans are insured by their agency

Frequently appraisers are required to defend their opinions as expert witnesses in a court of law. Utility companies also require a great deal of professional appraising service. Professional appraising firms are now often used for evaluating property for tax purposes, a task which was in many areas until recently performed by the elected tax assessors who may or may not have been professionally qualified.

When dealing with small local banks and savings and loans, the chances are the appraisers will be able to give you a fairly accurate value on a single family residence, particularly if it is a new speculative type single family residence. This is the type property with which they are most familiar and they will also have the benefit of comparisons with HUD appraisals in the area.

Don't be too disappointed, however, if they miss the target by a wide margin on commercial and industrial property, farmland, lake or mountain cottages, expensive residences, and so forth. If they don't know what a property is worth, the appraisal will likely be low. Many times you can overcome this through a meeting with the appraiser and lending officer when you back-up your request with facts. Sometimes pride or stubborness on the part of the appraiser may blow a good deal from you.

Several years ago I applied to a small savings and loan association for a loan on a mountain cottage and several acres of land. The appraiser, a conservative member of the firm's Board, set a value of $11,000. I sold the property within a year for $23,800. On another occasion I sold a house for $15,500 which I acquired a few days earlier for $13,000, and at the time of the sale I had an FHA commitment for $19,800. So, at best, appraising is not an exact science.

A real estate speculator dealing in small and medium-priced properties would soon be out of business if he attempted to make all of his purchases or sales on the basis of professional appraisals. A successful speculator is in fact a good appraiser himself of the type of properties in which he deals. He will recognize any situation where he might get in over his head and solicit the services of a professional.

There are three generally accepted approaches to estimating the value of property as follows:

1. *Comparable sales.* The property under consideration is compared as

to price, value, utility, and location; in relation to other similar property in the same neighborhood. This is the most common approach and the method best suited to the speculator. It should not, however, be the only consideration–particularly on income producing property.

Your primary interest when purchasing is forecasting the medium to long range value of the property. For this, you need a thorough knowledge of the area. What are the projected population figures? Does the area have a diversified industrial base? Can the property be rezoned to higher use? Will sewer lines be extended to the property? Is there a history of sound, progressive local government? Do you have an aggressive industrial agent constantly seeking new industry? Are major changes contemplated in highways? The answers to these and many other questions, too numerous to list, should be your guide as a speculator.

2. *Reproduction costs.* Sometimes referred to as replacement value. Using this method, you compare the cost of reproducing the improvements and add this to the land value–then deduct for applicable depreciation.
3. *Capitalization.* This approach is commonly used for income producing property with the conclusions double-checked by the comparable sales method and reproduction method.

   Using the capitalization process, value is established by consideration of the present and prospective future income of the property. This method can be rather tricky for the inexperienced. Advise with your accountant or a mortgage banker as to the worth of income property based upon capitalization.

Regardless of the approach used in estimating the value o property, when appraisals are made for loan purposes, the mora risk represented in the transaction should be considered. Thi phase of the risk, as separated from the physical risk involving th property itself, concerns the ability of the borrower to pay and hi desire or willingness to do so.

A loan can be defaulted rendering financial harm to the lende when the borrower finds himself unable to pay or simply becaus he is not sufficiently concerned with his obligation to be willing t pay. Careful analyzation of the borrower's financial statement including assets and liabilities and source(s) of income will indicat his ability, but the character of the borrower as determined by hi concern toward meeting his obligation promptly, must come fro a personal knowledge of the individual or a history of his credit obtained through personal references and a credit report.

In purchasing tracts it is usually wise to make your offer subject to an accurate survey, which will give you time to ascertain the exact amount of acreage you are buying. Some owners, however, will set a price on the tract and refuse to budge whether the survey reflects less acreage than stipulated in the deed. You may find yourself faced with this situation, along with the added disadvantage, that the owner has other prospects and will sell to the first person meeting his price. For this reason you should be able to estimate the acreage fairly accurately–taking out some of the risk or gamble. Use a 100 foot steel tape or a surveyor's chain for measuring, or if these are not available with a little experience you can get good ball park measurements by stepping off boundaries.

Computing Land Areas

Ascertain the area of parcels in the following manner:

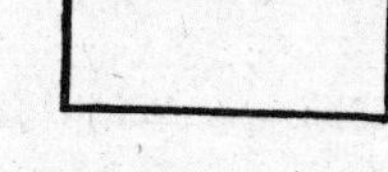

1. Rectangle tract. Multiply the length by the breadth.

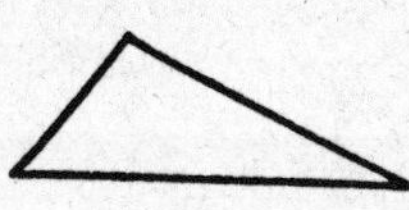

2. Triangular. Multiply the base by half the perpendicular height.

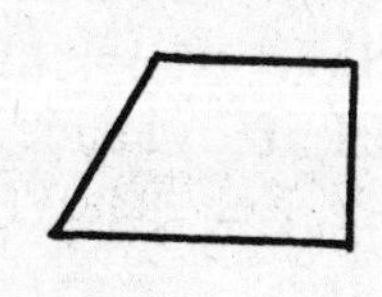

3. Trapezoid. (A four-sided tract having two of its sides parallel.) Multiply half the sum of the two parallel sides by the perpendicular distance between these sides.

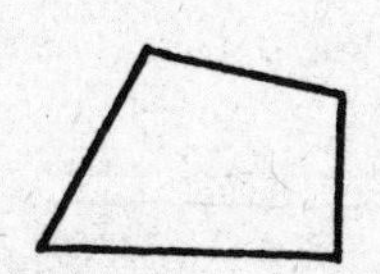

4. Trapezium. (Bounded by four straight lines which no two are paralleled to each other.) Divide the tract by lines into triangles and trapezoids. Ascertain the area of each and add together.

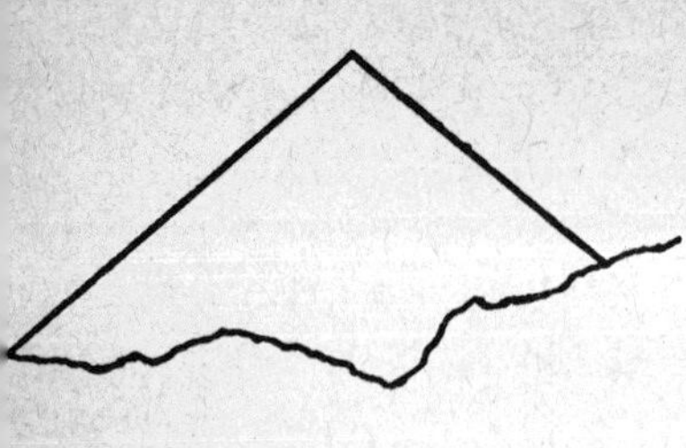

5. Land bounded by irregular objects such as stream, lake, or winding road. Draw a base line as close to the irregular boundary as possible. Draw numerous lines equidistant from each other from the base line to the irregular boundary line. Add the sum of all the intermediate lines to half the sum of the first line and last line and multiply the sum obtained by the distance between the lines. This will give you the area.

LAND MEASUREMENT TABLE

Acres	Square Feet
1	43,560
2	87,120
3	130,680
4	174,240
5	217,800
6	261,360
7	304,920
8	348,480
9	392,040
10	435,600

Note: For those interested in further information on appraising, I recommend McMichael's Appraising Manual by Stanley L. McMichael, Prentice-Hall, Inc., Englewood Cliffs, New Jersey.

17

FINANCING

Reliable sources for borrowing are essential to the speculator. A brief discussion of some of the more common sources follows:

Commercial Banks. As a general rule, consider commercial banks only as a source of short-term financing on improved property. Many of these are not allowed to lend on vacant land and in many instances they don't mind leaving the bulk of the real estate business to other institutions.

If, however, you have a good relationship with your local commercial banker this can be a tremendous asset. If you need to move quickly you may be able to acquire the "front end" money you need on your personal signature on a short-term basis–giving you time to liquidate other assets or make proper application to another institution for long-term mortgage money.

Depending on the ownership and management, these banks can vary from extremely conservative, to liberal in their lending policies. A good clue to this, is their ratio of loans to deposits. This percentage may run from the low 40's, for an ultra-conservative institution, to the high 70's in the more liberal ones. Average is probably around 60 per cent. Loans on improved real estate, other than HUD insured loans, are usually made on the basis of two-thirds of the appraised value and for five years or less.

Older bankers who experienced heavy losses on real estate loans in the depression of the 1930's may tend to be very cautious.

Recently liberalized regulations permit national banks to make amortized loans for as long as 30 years and for 90 per cent of value; however, most banks have a much more conservative policy. These restrictions do not apply to government-insured loans.

National banks are automatically approved as qualified HUD mortgagees, but some are not handling these insured loans because of red tape or because they can put their funds to a more profitable use elsewhere.

Savings and Loan Associations. S and L's have made a big impact on the mortgage lending business in recent years. The deposits in these institutions may equal or exceed those of commercial banks in some of the smaller communities. Nationwide assets exceed $100 billion dollars, about 85 per cent of which are in long-term mortgages.

All federally charter S and L's, and many state chartered associations, are members of the Federal Home Loan Bank system and subject to its supervision. This membership permits the individual S and L to borrow funds from its district Federal Home Loan Bank whenever funds are needed to pay off accounts of withdrawing members or to finance additional loans. Most associations are also members of the Federal Savings and Loan Insurance Corporation under which membership deposits are insured up to $20,000.

Present regulations permit Savings and Loans to make home mortgage loans up to 95 per cent of appraised value. This policy has, in some areas, reduced the number of HUD insured loans since the interest rates are often about the same and there is less red tape in closing an S and L loan. Many S and L's now make loans for as long as 30 years on new structures. An additional charge is levied against the borrower in the form of added discount on the higher ratio loans, and the interest rate may be slightly higher. For example, some associations will make a loan for 30 years on a new dwelling at a 7½ per cent interest rate and two points discount. However, on a ratio from 80 to 89 the interest is 7¾ per cent, with two and one-half points discount, and three points for loans from 90 to 95 per cent. The amount of the loan exceeding 80 per cent of the value is insured through a mortgage guaranty company.

Most Savings and Loans will make interim financing loans for builders and convert the loan to a permanent mortgage when the building is complete. Often you can avoid a double discount by using the same source for interim and permanent financing.

Life Insurance Companies. Assets of the nation's life insurance companies are around $165 billion. Life insurance companies get cash from the collection of premiums and investment of income. Premiums account for about 78 per cent of the total, as opposed to 22 per cent from investments. Real estate mortgages account for about 30 per cent of the industry's assets.

Generally, insurance companies process their loans either through branch insurance offices, located in the states in which they have been admitted to business, or through mortgage companies or loan correspondent brokers, who process the loan applications and then service these mortgage loans for a fee.

Insurance companies make conventional loans and participate heavily in HUD insured mortgages and government guaranteed GI loans.

Mortgage Companies. A large percentage of the permanent financing for single and multi-family housing is provided by major insurance companies represented locally by mortgage companies which originate loans. Mortgage companies usually represent several insurance companies and may at the same time represent one or more savings and loan associations and/or commercial banks.

These companies normally prefer government-backed mortgages, which can be moved readily to the secondary market or conventional mortgages on which they have advance purchase commitments.

These companies often service mortgages which they originate receiving an average of ½ to 1 per cent from the investor. A large volume of business is necessary to make this phase of the business profitable.

Most mortgage companies maintain a line of credit with a commercial bank–permitting them to close and warehouse loans, and advance money to the borrowers. The loans are then periodically transferred to a "permanent lender" such as New York Life Insurance Company, in volume lots perhaps one-half to a million dollars against a commitment made by the lender. To make sure the mortgage company is originating quality loans, the lender periodically sends a representative to the area to make spot checks.

The mortgage company receives an origination fee, averaging about 1 per cent on single family houses. This is collected at closing in the form of a discount. The amount of the total discount varies with the supply and demand of money and the type and quality of the loan. HUD limits the amount of discount which the borrower can pay to 1 per cent of the mortgage amount. Where a higher rate is charged, the seller must pay the additional amount.

If the discount is 5 per cent and the loan is approved in the amount of $30,000, this means the borrower will actually receive $28,500. Normally, 1 per cent of the discount (in this case $300) is retained by the mortgage company as an origination fee. The lender would in turn be discounting the loan by 4 per cent (points) and would actually be purchasing the $30,000 loan used in our illustration for $28,800.

The advent of government insured and guaranteed loans, coupled with the liberalization of laws permitting banks and insurance companies in one state to acquire mortgage loans made in other states, has created a substantial need for mortgage companies.

Standardization of mortgage loan practices, initiated years ago by FHA through the agency's insuring regulations, has contributed much to the liquidity and/or negotiability of mortgages.

Secondary mortgage markets are discussed in a separate topic under HUD.

Regulations governing qualifications for a HUD mortgagee may be obtained in any HUD office. They relate primarily to the financial capability and moral character of the person(s) desiring to qualify.

Individual Lenders. Almost every community has persons with money who will invest in first mortgages. Often you may be able to get a better interest rate or a higher loan to value ratio, than through the established lending agencies. The disadvantage of depending on individuals is that capital will be limited and financial circumstances of the individual changes often. Entering into a transaction on the assumption of this source of money can be risky.

By and large, I have found individuals most helpful on loans which do not meet bank standards, but are often perfectly good loans. Some individuals also make second mortgage loans, charging sufficient interest to offset the added risk and weak liquidity factors.

Farm Loans. See discussion in the Chapter on "Buying Farm Property."

18

ADVERTISING

Advertising expenses for real estate speculators are usually very nominal. Many properties are sold without using the generally accepted mediums such as newspaper, radio, and television.

In another sense there is perhaps always some form of advertising applied because it is essential for prospective purchasers to know a property is for sale and important to the owner that they be impressed favorably.

On raw property I have found the best advertising to be changing the appearance of the land. If it is grown up in weeds and scrub timber, get rid of this rubbish and sow it to grass. Fill in gullies and remove surface rock. These things attract more attention than signs all over the property.

On most properties I have sold, without using a broker, I have not spent a penny on formal advertising. On a few, I have placed a "for sale" sign on the property along with my telephone number. Occasionally I have used a classified newspaper ad.

If you have bought the property at a bargain, improved the appearance, and let some of the neighbors know you would consider selling it, this may be all the advertising you need. If you live in a small or medium-sized community you will likely already know your best prospects. A few telephone or personal calls may be all that is needed.

If the property is "cold" and not attracting sufficient interest, you perhaps should wait another year for transitions in the neighborhood making it more appealing to buyers. If you are determined to move it now, and have tried the above approaches–list it with a broker at a reasonable price with the understanding that he will push it and advertise it widely.

Never leave a "for sale" sign on a piece of property for extended periods of time. I know parcels of property now that have had "for sale" signs up for two or three years or longer. I assume these properties are overpriced or someone would have bought them during this time, consequently I seldom inquire about them.

Bulletin boards in factories or offices are good places to advertise residential property and since they are free, may be worthwhile on vacant property.

I have a friend who has bought and sold millions of dollars worth of speculative real estate and I have never seen a sign on property he has for sale other than when he lists with a broker. He operates in the small city in which he lives and surrounding small communities. He has a reputation for buying right and dealing in good property. He has a wide acquaintance of people who trade in real estate and usually either sells to them or gets his leads on prospects from them.

Advertisement by a broker or agent is an entirely different matter. It is one of his largest expenses and the life blood of his business. He is forever striving to improve his advertisements in a manner to get more attention for less money. He needs regular advertising, not only to make sales but to secure listings. Many people ready to list a house in a larger community do not know a broker personally and make the selection based on advertisements which have impressed them either in quality or quantity, or both.

Raw land speculators are basically wholesalers and wholesalers in most businesses require much less advertising than retailers.

Newspaper, television, and radio advertising is best used on commodities that appeal to the masses or at least a relatively large group of people. A single family residence or perhaps a condominium would fall into this category, but a warehouse or large tract of land for development would not. If you live in a small community, say less than 10,000 people, your worthwhile prospects may be limited to 25 persons or less. In a large metropolitan area the situation would be different and if a sign on the property won't get the job done, you probably should use the services of a broker.

19

BROKERAGE

A full discussion of brokerage is not merited here but there are at least two reasons why a brief discussion of the topic is warranted:

1. Some knowledge of the brokerage business may assist you in using the services of your broker in a more profitable manner.
2. Speculation in real estate could lead you to become interested in full-time brokerage.

Previously, anyone had the right to act as agent, solicit listings, negotiate deals for clients, give advice, and so forth, however, brokers are now licensed and regulated under state laws which have been enacted to safeguard the public from incompentency and sometimes dishonesty.

Licensing Laws

Licensing laws vary from state to state but generally speaking they require an individual to be of good moral character, to take and pass a comprehensive examination, and to have experience in the real estate business prior to receiving a broker's license.

Experience is gained by first obtaining a salesman's license under a sponsoring broker, after having passed the required salesman's examination, and working as a salesman for one or more years as the law may require. Most state licensing commissions will supply any persons desiring to become a salesman, a handbook of information on which the examination is based. In addition, the Commission may refer you to other more comprehensive texts. An annual license fee is required from both salesman and brokers.

Brokers are usually referred to as agents and represent a "principal," either the purchaser or seller, in dealing with a third party. Brokers may not represent buyer and seller in the same transaction and collect a commission from each without the knowledge and consent of both parties.

Most states do not require a broker to have a listing in writing and signed in order to negotiate a sale or exchange but a careful broker will insist on a signed listing with terms and conditions carefully spelled out before acting as agent.

Commissions

Brokers earn their livelihood through commissions. Some persons who sell property through brokers feel commission charges are excessive. They do not realize the risk or gamble accepted by the agent.

A broker has the expense of an office, advertising, and his own time. He expends considerable energy and money on many properties he never sells, consequently, he must get paid well when he successfully negotiates a transaction.

The amount of commission charged varies from area to area but 6 per cent is about average for residential and other improved property and 10 per cent is customary in many areas for vacant land, particularly for large tracts and farms where much time is required to show the property.

Often a broker will list new houses and sell for a commission of from 2 to 4 per cent. This is especially true if he has an exclusive listing on an entire subdivision where he may promote "open houses" and possibly sign contracts of sale on several houses in one day.

Salesmen's compensation are negotiated between broker and salesman. The salesman usually receives about 40 per cent of the brokerage commission for selling a property and perhaps as much as 60 per cent if he is both the listing agent and selling agent.

Multiple Listings

Brokers in many communities have a multiple listing arrangement, whereby, when a property is listed, it is made available to all members of the multiple listing service for showing and selling. The commission is divided according to terms agreed upon for members of the multiple listing service with a portion going to the listing broker, a portion to the selling broker, and a small percentage to the multiple listing service. Usually about 70 per cent goes to the selling broker, 20 per cent to the listing broker, and 10 per cent to the multiple listing service for expense and overhead.

Net Listings and Open Listings

Normally, brokers are not permitted to accept net listings, whereby the seller agrees to accept a stipulated amount with the broker retaining all he can get in excess of this amount. This type of listing opens the door to misunderstandings and greed, and often leave questions as to whether the seller's best interests were represented.

Most listings are on an exclusive agency or broker basis for a stipulated period of time. Under open listings, which are not acceptable to many brokers, the owner retains the right to list the property with other brokers or sell it himself. The sale of the property terminates the listing and the broker making the sale receives a commission, but if the owner sells the property he has no obligation for commission.

A broker must be employed by the one for whom he acts in order to be entitled to a commission under the law. Employment should be in writing but need not be unless the law in his state required it. He is entitled to his commission when he has performed the service for which he is employed.

Pros and Cons of the Brokerage Business

Like most any other business, real estate brokerage can be rewarding to the individual willing to devote the time and energy to learn it and to sacrifice income during the beginning years for greater rewards once you have an established business.

Often failures occur in real estate brokerage as the result of persons entering the field because they cannot find other satisfactory employment. Real estate brokerage is very competitive and only the aggressive, energetic, and well-informed will survive or at least reach any measure of success. This is no place for the nine-to-five worker. Many contracts are signed by brokers after his neighbors have gone to bed. You must meet the schedule of your customers who may only be able to look at property on weekends or after normal working hours.

Women are coming more and more into prominence as salesmen and brokers, and seem to be especially adept at residential selling. Many housewives have the final say on purchasing a home, and women salesmen are better able to recognize and point out features influencing the housewife.

Some brokers engage in speculation as a side line but this can get to be a questionable practice, particularly on his own listings since the broker is representing both the seller and purchaser and the temptation is too great to beat the seller down on price rather than make an all out effort to get a fair price. By all means, the seller should be informed by the broker that he is interested in making an offer on the property before accepting a listing.

Do not attempt to start a real estate brokerage business and engage in speculation at the same time unless you have a lot of capital. Getting a new real estate brokerage business to break-even point is enough challenge in itself and I wouldn't recommend counting on the income for meeting payments on property I had purchased on an installment basis.

Under any circumstances, prior to going into the brokerage business, ascertain the total volume of real estate transactions in the area where you will operate. I have seen small communities where the number of brokers were out of proportion to the total real estate business, and by simple mathematics it was easy to determine there was no way for all to survive if the business was split equally. This does not prove that a few well-established firms are not doing well. It does mean you would be taking a greater than normal risk in starting a new business.

Part II

Higher Use—The Speculators Market

20

SINGLE FAMILY RESIDENCES

Buying and selling single family residences is among the least profitable real estate endeavors. An exception may occur when the speculator has the time and ability to repair an older house with his own labor. Also there may be profit opportunities when an owner must sell quickly at a financial sacrifice.

Many older houses come on the market at prices which appear very tempting, even when you contemplate the necessity of employing a contractor to do the modernizing. Invariably, however, these costs will exceed your estimates. Unless you are restoring a house for your own home, where profit is not the prime consideration, I suggest you avoid this temptation.

There are situations where you can profit by moving a house which is in the way of a new highway or other public projects and can buy the structure for next to nothing. Even this situation can be tricky. I have seen individuals take losses on moving perfectly good houses donated to them by the owner. The time and expense of getting permits, power and telephone lines disconnected, buying, grading and landscaping your lot, constructing your foundation, hooking up utilities, repairing damages incurred in moving, and redecorating will likely be greater than you anticipate.

In contemplating buying new or recently constructed houses for resale, there are several forces working against you. First of all, you will be competing for sales with every speculative builder in your community and these people normally work on a high volume, low margin, basis. Secondly, your superior judgment as to value will be worth little since your customers and half of the neighboring property owners will know the value, based upon HUD appraisals of similar property in the area. Next, you will find, the key to selling single family residences is arranging financing in a manner to keep the required equity and monthly payments as low as possible. Competing brokers will likely be more knowledgable in this field than you.

Selling land for single family development is another matter and offers many opportunities for profit in most communities. You may even want to consider the possibilities of subdividing if you have a tract in an area where minimum standards apply. (See Chapter on Subdividing Residential Property)

21

APARTMENTS, CONDOMINIUMS AND COOPERATIVES

Apartment construction is sweeping the country like a grass fire. As an example, many city building inspectors report, while less than 10 per cent of their residential permits were for apartments in 1960, more than 50 per cent of the permits issued in 1972 were for apartments.

Reasons for More Apartments

There are numerous reasons why apartments are gaining favor with American families. Some are:

1. Increase in price of building lots.
2. Increased interest rates, higher discounts and closing costs, and skyrocketing construction costs have put the purchase of single family houses out of the reach of many.
3. Labor is scarce and expensive for ground maintenance and building upkeep.
4. Population is more transient.
5. Home ownership has weakened as a symbol of stability and solidarity.
6. Increasing concentration of population in metropolitan centers.

With suburbia moving further and further out, the expense and time required getting to and from work becomes ever more burdensome, consequently many families may choose to become apartment dwellers closer in and settle for the luxury of open spaces on weekends at a cottage in the country.

Notwithstanding the Government's commitment toward making home ownership a goal within reach of most families, a single family home may become more and more a luxury for the middle-aged and well fixed family.

One factor looming on the horizon, which could further accelerate the growing number of apartments, is the possibility of gasoline rationing. This would make far out suburban living with the necessity of two or more cars per family less attractive.

Duplex or Fourplex Worth Considering

For a young couple getting started a duplex or fourplex with one unit for owner-occupancy is worth investigating. Generous financing can usually be arranged if you are going to live in one apartment and manage the others. I know one young couple who started four years ago with a duplex and now own ten units with more being planned. They are operating with no capital reserves and could be wiped out with a serious vacancy rate or competition from lower prices. On the other hand with continuing rising costs, they may "have it made" in another 10 to 15 years.

There are numerous examples of those who have pyramided a modest investment to significant wealth in the apartment business during the last 20 years. High leveraging and good management have been their keys to success. Their ability to increase rents due to inflation and rising costs of new construction has also contributed to their progress.

What Size Project?

Where management and maintenance are not supplied by the owner, arriving at an economical number of units is important. If, however, you are prepared to do your own management and maintenance there is no minimum number.

Many consider the minimum number of units for an investor who contemplates hiring a resident manager to be 75 to 100. A lesser number may justify full-time management, particularly if it is a luxury complex where both the tenants and the buildings and grounds require more tender love and care.

The more units which can be used in prorating the cost of amenities, such as swimming pools, shuffleboard courts, tennis courts, saunas, and so forth, the better. For a 30-unit apartment complex, a $15,000 pool adds $500 to the cost of each unit, but for 100 units the pool would add only $150 per unit, or a slightly larger pool could be built for $20,000–adding $200 to the cost of each unit.

From the management/maintenance standpoint, a project keeping a man and wife team busy full time is very desirable. For moderate size, moderate price apartments, this number should be from 75 to 125 units.

Expense/Income Ratio

The expense to income ratio should fall between 30 per cent and 40 per cent based on a 95 per cent occupancy. This rate of occupancy is commonly used by lenders but many conservative lenders and owners believe it to be dangerously high since a cash flow of 6 or 7 per cent coupled with depreciation benefits, is generally needed to make a project acceptable to the owner.

Supplying the Land

The apartment boom during the last decade has made a lot of money for a lot of land owners, investors, and speculators.

A tract of land having a value of $3,000 an acre when used for single family dwellings may be worth $10,000 to $20,000 an acre for multi-family purposes. This is due to the increased density ranging anywhere from 5 to 25 units per acre for garden or townhouse type apartments.

Land development can be a big factor in making an apartment project feasible and consequently the builder can pay considerably more for a near ideal parcel of land than for one on which the development costs are high. In most areas the cost of land development for garden or town house projects will usually vary from around $1,000 per unit on the low side to $3,000 to $5,000 a unit on the high side. I have been involved in apartment projects over the last few years and have encountered development costs as low as $400 per unit and as high as $4,000 per unit.

With such a wide variation of development costs brought about mainly by the "quality" of the land–it is easy to see why a builder can pay much more for land which offers fewer problems in the way of grading, filling, drainage, rock blasting, retaining walls, and so forth.

There is much land suitable for single family dwellings using large lots, individual septic tanks, and drain field lines which would be unsatisfactory for multi-family projects. Apartment complexes require a location on a city or utility company sewer line, or the installation and maintenance of an expensive sewer treatment system by the developer.

Apartment developers usually encounter two major problems in finding suitable land. The first is finding desirable property at a reasonable price, and the second is getting the land zoned for high density use. Zoning requests for higher density use are meeting more and more resistance in many areas. Protests generally come from neighbors who object to increased traffic, crowding of neighborhood schools, and the fear of an adverse effect on the value of their homes. In some instances the zoning is being denied–in others the developer is forced to lower his proposed density, provide more parking space, playground area, and so forth.

In larger densely-populated areas, hi-rise apartments are widely used. Often these are in the high priced or luxury class and occupied by older couples, widows, widowers, or bachelor men and women. They are not desirable for families with children since they do not have ample recreation space and the older tenants object to the noise and congestion. Hi-rise projects can be located on choice close in land since the developer can often get 100 units or more per acre depending on height restrictions. Price for this may be $50,000 to $100,000 an acre and much more in some areas.

Swinging Singles

A popular type apartment complex has come into prominence in recent years and is referred to as "swinging singles." They are usually replete with numerous amenities including pool, tennis courts, sauna baths, and are designed in such a manner to afford the tenants a great amount of privacy. "Swinging adults" apartments are similar in nature, but do not require the tenants to have single status; however, families with children are not permitted.

Financing

Apartment financing may come from any number of sources but money for most large complexes come from insurance companies and the loans are usually originated by mortgage bankers. Many smaller complexes are financed by savings and loan associations. For more information see Chapter on "Financing."

Condominiums and Cooperatives

Cooperative type apartments, usually of the hi-rise variety, gained immense popularity in California and Florida several years ago and are now common throughout the country.

The condominium concept of ownership, while relatively new to this country, may have originated some 2500 years ago in Rome. At any rate, it has been used extensively in Europe, Latin America, and Puerto Rico for a long time.

Under this concept, single units in a multiunit structure are individually owned. The owner of the single living unit shares ownership of halls, stairs, grounds, driveways, elevators, roof, lobbies, and so forth.

The cooperative apartment differs from a condominium in several ways, the chief distinction being the cooperative tenant owns outright a prorated percentage of the building(s) and grounds and holds possession of his living unit under a long time renewable lease.

Under either concept the project may consist of one building or several. They may be hi-rise, garden or town house apartments, single family structures; or any combination of these.

Condominiums, Cooperatives—Compared

Other differences include the following:

1. In condominiums, individuals take title to their units. In cooperatives, each one owns stock or membership in the cooperative and has the right to live in one of the units.
2. In condominiums, individuals vote on a proportional basis. In cooperatives, each member has one vote no matter what the size of his unit.
3. In condominiums, individuals are taxed separately on their units. In cooperatives, they pay their share of taxes on the project in their monthly carrying charges.
4. In condominiums, individuals may or may not have mortgages on their own units, depending on their wishes and their ability to finance the purchase of their units. In cooperatives, the mortgage covers all the units and the members are not free to exclude their units from the cooperative mortgage.

Advantages Listed by HUD

The Department of Housing and Urban Development lists the following advantages of cooperatives and condominiums to owners:

1. *Hedge Against Inflation:* The housing project is operated on a nonprofit basis. The owners pay monthly, only their share of the project's actual operating costs. Thus, increases in the monthly housing cost are limited to actual increases in operating costs. In rental housing, the rent is often affected by supply and demand. Thus, during times of housing shortage or general inflation, rents may be increased in uncontrolled rental projects even though the landlord's operating costs may not have been significantly increased.
2. *Tax Advantages:* An owner may deduct from his income for Federal Income Tax purposes (and often for State Income Tax purposes too) the real estate taxes and mortgage interest he has paid during the year. (In a cooperative, the member

deducts his share of the real estate taxes and mortgage interest paid by the cooperative corporation.) A cooperative or condominium owner, thus, has basically the same income tax advantage as a conventional homeowner. This, in effect, is a reduction in the owner's housing cost.

3. *Absence of Landlord's Profit:* Inasmuch as the owners are their own landlord and since they operate on a nonprofit basis, their monthly housing cost does not include an allocation for landlord's profit which is included in the rent of an ordinary tenant. This in itself may amount to a reduction of 10 per cent or more in monthly housing costs.
4. *Reduced Maintenance Expense:* Experience has shown that owners take better care of the overall property than tenants. Moreover, the owners frequently handle the redecoration of their unit's interior on a do-it-yourself basis. Maintenance costs are, therefore, usually less in a cooperative or condominium project than in a rental development.

Condominiums Most Popular

While cooperatives have been around in this country a lot longer, the condominium is now the popular approach. This is perhaps in part because the condominium owner can sell without permission of other owners and if he has his unit paid for, or mortgage current, he cannot be foreclosed upon even if units of other owners are in distress. Conceivably the tenant of a cooperative could lose his apartment if the corporation failed to pay its taxes.

Under either the cooperative or condominium concept, the individual pays his proportionate share of maintenance and management costs.

Conventional Financing

Condominium developers may use either "conventional" financing or if the project qualifies, may obtain a HUD insured mortgage. Most developers are currently using conventional financing. The reasons are primarily twofold.

1. It eliminates much of the red tape and expedites the project.
2. Many projects are luxury or semi-luxury and HUD insured mortgages cover less of the value as the price of the units increase.

HUD Insured Financing

HUD insures mortgages, obtained by investors, to finance construction or rehabilitation of housing projects of four or more single-family units.

Later, the individual units in such projects are released from the blanket mortgage, sold to individual owners, and financed separately. The single units, when sold, may be financed by the buyers with HUD-insured or non-HUD mortgages, or a buyer may purchase on an all-cash basis without a mortgage if he chooses to do so.

Whether the project is new or existing, sale to condominium buyers can be made only after HUD has processed the case and found the plan of condominium ownership acceptable.

The extent of interest the owner of a living unit has in the common areas and facilities is governed by the ratio of value of his unit to the total value of all the units. This ratio also represents his voting interest in the condominium owners' association. Along with the owners of other units in the project, he has the right to use the common areas and facilities and the obligation to maintain them. The owners make monthly contributions to the condominium association covering their proportionate share of the cost of maintaining these common areas and facilities.

HUD's commitment to insure the individual mortgages is based on these conditions:

1. All planned construction must be completed.
2. Units amounting to 80 per cent of the value of all units must have been sold to HUD-approved buyers.
3. The mortgage on a family unit must be a first mortgage.

One person may own as many as four units financed with HUD-insured mortgages, provided he lives in one of them. It is not required that all of the unit mortgages be HUD-insured. Some of the unit mortgages may be HUD-insured, some financed conventionally, and others purchased for cash.

The project may include commercial and community facilities adequate to serve the people who live in the project.

This program, like other HUD programs, includes certain rules for the proper protection and management of the project.

Family Unit Mortgage Limitations

The following limits apply to the mortgage on a single unit:

1. The interest rate cannot exceed current established HUD rate. The HUD mortgage insurance premium is ½ of 1 per cent a year on decreasing principal balances without taking into account prepayments or delinquencies.
2. The mortgage term can be no less than 10 years nor more than 30 years (35 years in some cases, with HUD approval).
3. The mortgage amount cannot exceed $33,000. The amount is further limited as follows:
   a. Based on the HUD value of the family unit including common areas and facilities, it cannot exceed 97 per cent of the first $15,000, plus 90 per cent of the next $10,000, plus 80 per cent of the value above $25,000 for an owner-occupant.
   b. For a unit owned by a person who does not live in it, the mortgage amount cannot exceed 80 per cent of the amount computed for an owner-occupant.

The price a developer can pay for land for a cooperative or condominium depends upon location and density. In a low-rise, low-density project in a smaller city he might be limited to $1,000 per unit or less. But five or ten times this much might be reasonable for a Miami Beach hi-rise.

Land requirements for cooperatives or condominiums are similar to requirements for rental apartment units.

22

SHOPPING CENTERS

No other single factor can compare with the economic influence of shopping centers on American cities since World War II.

Since development of shopping centers particularly regional enters is a job for professionals, your interest as a land speculator s limited to the influence which centers exert over property you nay contemplate buying or selling. The two primary factors which ropagated the shopping center boom are:

1. Mushrooming of residential housing in the suburbs.
2. Downtown traffic congestion created by the greater use of a greater number of automobiles by employees and shoppers.

Counting regional neighborhood and community centers, there re close to 15,000 in existence and the numbers are still climbing. hopping centers have an annual sales volume of close to 140 illion dollars and account for nearly 50 per cent of all retail trade n this country.

It is contemplated that by 1975 more than half of the nations etail sales will take place in shopping centers.

eal Estate Values Influenced

Large regional centers may completely reshuffle the real estate alue of an entire city and its environs. Some of the larger centers ave 100 or more stores with parking for 10,000 or more cars. The current trend is to bigness but the fact remains that 90 per cent of all shopping centers are of the smaller community or neighborhood type.

Keep in mind as a speculator that usually property values will rise tremendously surrounding regional centers and the influence of the center will depress downtown property.

Fortunes have been made in raw land by those with inside information on when and where new shopping centers were to be located and by some who, without the lack of inside information, accurately predicted the coming of a major center based on growth patterns of the area.

I have seen raw land prices adjacent to centers jump from $2,000 an acre to $20, $30, and $40 thousand dollars an acre in a three-year period. I have also witnessed downtown property dropping in value more than 50 per cent as a result of a suburban regional center.

Regional centers usually pivot around two or three large department stores such as Sears, J. C. Penneys, and often the leading independent store in the city and, of course, the major drug and grocery chains followed by dozens of small shops.

Cost of Space

Large department stores, supermarkets, and so forth usually pay from $1.50 to $2.00 per square foot per annum for their space. Usually the developer also ties his rental take to gross sales requiring the tenant to pay a fixed minimum or a percentage of the gross—whichever is higher.

Smaller stores may pay as high as eight to ten dollars per square foot. Centers are often contructed on ground-leased property. A well-located, properly leased, and efficiently managed shopping center can represent the most rewarding of all real estate developments. Profits run from 13 per cent to 18 per cent a year.

23

INDUSTRIAL REAL ESTATE

As a rule, industrial land requires a heavy investment coupled with a high nonliquidity factor.

Most of our industry was once primarily centered in the northeast and north central United States but much of the industrial growth in recent years has been in the South, Southwest, South Central, and Pacific regions.

In the past, industrial property did not offer great attraction to the speculator since potential users were limited and turnover was slow. More recently, however, the migration of industry, the moving from central city to suburbia, and the requirement for new, more modern facilities has generated profitable activity in this field.

When new industry migrates to your community, or existing ones expand, nine chances out of ten it will be to a suburban or outlining area (not in the central city) and the new facility will be a one-story building located on a rather large tract leaving room for future expansion.

Many communities now employ an Industrial Agent for the purpose of enticing new plants to locate within their environs. He may be employed by a city, a county, a chamber of commerce, or a nonprofit industrial committee composed of community-spirited citizens. He in turn will likely be working with a regional or state industrial agency and in many instances with railroad industrial development departments. Making his acquaintance is important.

Some major railroads employ as many as 150 people in economic development work in an effort to generate more business on their line.

WAREHOUSING

Opportunities are greater for the average speculator in land for warehousing than in manufacturing real estate. This is one area where you may become a developer in order to profit on your land while taking little risk.

The ideal situation is to find a "triple A" tenant who needs a warehouse and will contract with you to build same and lease for 15 years or longer. Given this situation, you should have no trouble in arranging 100 per cent financing and your only real expenditure could be the time expended in putting the deal together.

Speculative Buildings

Numerous contractors specialize in warehouse buildings (particularly shell steel buildings) and you can obtain a turnkey price without difficulty. Unfortunately, however, these opportunities do not come along often since "triple A" companies are likely to seek out landlords who are experienced in building and leasing warehousing. There is an alternative approach. You can build a "speculative" warehouse. This business which was once considered by many to be too risky is catching on more and more, and once you have sufficient experience you may want to consider a speculative warehouse. I have one friend who concentrated on building apartments for years but has now switched almost completely to speculative warehousing.

A friendly banker and a lot of courage are necessary for participation in the speculative warehouse business. This is particularly true of your first venture. Appraisers are often generous enough to enable you to finance 100 per cent of your cost. Bankers are reluctant, however, to loan money on a structure where no definite commitment for its use exists. Consequently obtaining financing for speculative warehousing will depend more on the financial statement and moral character of the borrower than the physical facility to be pledged for security. Pledging other assets or taking in a financial partner are the approaches used by most borrowers.

Speculative warehouses are usually (but not always) steel shell buildings. The most popular sizes seem to range in the category of from 30,000 to 50,000 square feet.

Erection is normally done by a contractor who specializes in this business. Buildings are erected on a concrete slab usually either four or six inches thick. The slab can be omitted and poured after a tenant is secured. This cuts down the cost but has other disadvantages which will be explained later.

In most areas, buildings should be insulated and sprinkled. Lighting, heating, and plumbing are usually left to the tenant. The same applies to office space, partitions, and so forth. A small parking area is gravelled with the paving left to the tenant.

The above items vary from area to area and speculator to speculator but my research indicates the above to be average. Construction time should be four months or less for a 50,000 square feet shell building.

Most warehouse speculators want a land ratio of about two to one. For a 40,000 square foot warehouse, you would need about two acres. Annual rents for warehouse space vary from about 70 cents to $4.50 per square foot per annum. The cost of construction usually varies from $3 to $6 per square foot depending upon the area. Land costs for prime sites are usually $10,000 to to $20,000 an acre.

Your search for tenants should begin shortly after you start construction. The ideal tenant is one who is strong financially, willing to pay a reasonable rent, and take a long lease.

If by the time your construction is almost through you do not have a tenant lined up, start looking for tenants who need temporary storage facilities on short term arrangements. Rent portions of the space to several tenants if necessary. Keep these leases short so you can get the building vacated when you find a good tenant for the entire space.

Obviously, this business is risky. The mortgage payments will have to be coughed up every month whether the building is rented or not. On the surface it would seem stupid to erect a structure which takes only three or four months, then look for a tenant.

Why not just advertise you have the land and will build to suit the tenant? This is quite often done but with much less success. There are clients available, both warehousing and manufacturing, who are interested in an existing building, only.

While in the industrial recruiting business, I lost several good prospects because our community did not have existing vacant space for lease. We always tried to switch them to a landowner who would gladly erect a building in a short period of time and enter into a reasonable lease. Usually, however, they located in another community where the facility was existing.

Also, local and state industrial commissions serve, free of charge, as sales agents for existing facilities. Many state agencies keep an inventory of available manufacturing space in every community and pass this information along to industrial prospects.

Financing is usually from 10 to 20 years on a shell industrial building. If your credit is strong and/or if you have a good track record in this field, you can expect to get 100 per cent financing in many communities if you build efficiently. Banks usually lend from 65 to 75 per cent of appraised value, but appraisals normally run high in relationship to replacement costs.

How One Speculator Finances Warehouses

I know one individual who has been in this business for several years and normally borrows about 150 per cent of his cost of land and buildings. His initial loan is short term. He gets an appraisal of five to six dollars per square foot and borrows around 75 per cent of this amount. His construction costs, including land, run around three dollars a square foot.

Initial money for construction is borrowed on short-term and carried on this basis until he gets a permanent tenant, at which time he rearranges his financing and assigns his lease as collateral. After a good lease and permanent financing is obtained, he sells most of his projects to investors who can benefit from both the cash flow and depreciation.

INDUSTRIAL PARKS

Development of industrial parks is an expensive undertaking and requires a great deal of expertise. Your best opportunities may be in assembling the land for this purpose, then selling it to a developer. If actual development is contemplated, find a joint-venture partner who has successful experience in this field.

Until recently an unwelcome neighbor, many communities are now wooing industrial parks into the suburbs as a new source of tax revenue. More than 80 per cent of today's planned industrial parks have come into existence since World War II.

Thorough Planning and Ample Time Essential

Total development of a park may take from six to twelve years. For this reason anyone venturing into this field must consider his long range financial stability along with his development/construction capabilities. Actually the mechanics are not too different from those applied to single family subdivisions. The idea is to buy a large tract of land or assemble smaller tracts at wholesale prices, improve it, then sell smaller parcels at retail.

Proper zoning and service from all necessary utilities including rail, if possible, are prerequisite. Reasonable land costs and land that requires a minimum amount of cuts or fills are important.

A feasibility study is essential and you will need adequate long-term financing. In contrast to a residential subdivision, which you would likely expect to market in one to three years, you may be looking at 10 or 15 years for an industrial park.

Generally speaking, sites in industrial parks have better acceptance than single sites. Community-sponsored development foundations will usually give you a lot of support, however, in some instance these agencies become nonprofit developers and may be your competition.

If a park is being developed in your community you may want to consider buying a lot or two in the very early stages of development. After several buildings are in the park you will have an excellent chance for land appreciation, much better than on residential lots, although you may have to hold longer.

Examples of Profits on Industrial Parks

Three years ago I optioned a large tract of land at $1,500 an acre for a public housing project. The site was turned down by the Department of Housing and Urban Development and I moved the project to another site.

The land was subsequently converted into an industrial park and has been completely sold out at prices between $10,000 and $30,000 an acre.

My mistake was in not reading the growth pattern signs of the area. Sewers have recently been installed and shortly after my option expired, an 80-store regional shopping mall was announced close by and the entire area blossomed with new development. Industrial parks normally require much more time.

Obviously the developer, who picked up the land at $1,500 an acre, spent a lot of time and money in upgrading the property but a speculator could have easily doubled or tripled his money on buying and selling the raw land.

The ideal industrial park site is a large tract of properly zoned, reasonably priced, gently rolling land, located at an interstate highway interchange and bounded by a railroad siding. The problem is these situations are non-existent.

Price of Industrial Land

I questioned industrial realtors in 18 major cities across the country regarding industrial land prices. The range was from $10,000 to $50,000 per acre for good sites—properly zoned and served by necessary utilities, highways, and rail. These realtors estimated 1960 prices on this same land in a range from $2,000 to $10,000 per acre. Current prices were most commonly quoted in the $10,000 to $20,000 an acre range.

A national building trade magazine reported recently that industrially zoned land in Cleveland, Ohio is priced at $22,000 to

$27,000 an acre on the east side and $37,000 to $45,000 on the west side of the city. Industrially zoned land within the city was listed at from $35,000 to $50,000 an acre.

24

MOBILE HOMES

Still in its infancy, and often controversial, the mobile home industry now occupies a very important place in housing the nation's families.

Many communities have taken somewhat of a "be quiet and it will go away" attitude toward the industry. Others have attempted to outlaw mobile homes altogether and some have accepted them on a piece meal basis–often using a consent of the surrounding property holders approach, to granting permits. More progressive communities have recognized mobile homes are with us in large and growing numbers, and burying our heads in the sand will not solve the problems accompanying their use. They have established reasonable regulations governing the zoning, construction, and operation of mobile home parks and subdivisions.

Until recently, many thought the modular or factory built house would take a big percentage of the mobile home business, and while undoubtedly industrialized housing will grow, the record to date is one of more failures than successes, both among the "shade tree operators" and the giant conglomerates.

Most mobile homes today are not very mobile at all and detractors question whether they are homes at all. Be that as it may, however, these units are accounting for upwards of 95 per cent of all new housing priced below $15,000.

Some trace their origin back to 1923 when the first modern home-on-wheels was designed by black students at Virginia's Hampton Institute.

The industry did not gain much momentum until after World War II, when many veterans and their young families, students and otherwise, began using "trailers" as a stop-gap measure to substitute for conventional housing, which was not available or was priced out of their reach.

Why Mobiles Sell

Young families on limited budgets still account for a large percentage of mobile home sales. These are some of the reasons for their appeal to this group:

1. Low down payment.
2. Furniture can be included in down payment and amortization.
3. Monthly payments may be less than rent for suitable conventional housing.
4. Many apartment owners exclude children.
5. Mobile housing is readily available.
6. Home can follow the family from college to first job, or from interim or temporary employment to the next position.
7. Mobile units serve as a stop-gap residence in a new city until determination is made where to build or buy and in what price range.

Who Uses Mobiles—and Where?

Next to young families, the second greatest demand for mobile homes is from retired or semi-retired, constituting from 20 to 25 per cent of users. Large numbers of mobiles for this purpose are concentrated in Florida, Arizona, Southern California and other popular retirement areas, but they are used to some extent throughout the nation, often with Mom and Pop turning the home place over to son or daughter, for his or her family, and moving into a mobile home on the back of the lot.

On the basis of new titles issued, there were 56,989 mobile homes purchased in Florida in 1972—an increase of 58 per cent over 1970. With 3,000 dealers and 3,000 parks, the Gator state has led the nation in registration of mobile homes for several years.

Trends Toward Luxury

Today's mobile has little in common with the eight or ten foot wide linoleum floored Spartan trailer of the late 1940's. Most mobiles are at least 12 feet wide and some are 14 feet wide. Many are expandable. Then there are the double wides which may offer you 1,200 to 1,400 square feet of living space or more, often with three or four bedrooms and two or more baths.

The more luxurious models have increased in numbers and indicates a wider acceptance on the part of more mature families. It is not at all unusual to find doctors, lawyers, and businessmen occupying mobiles, particularly in the Florida, California, and Arizona areas where these units have gained such wide acceptance.

Mobiles Have Their Drawbacks

Despite the wide use, mobiles still have many drawbacks and certainly their share of detractors. The mobile home decreases in value far more rapidly than the conventional home. Also they are more vulnerable to destruction by floods, hurricanes, fires, and other natural disasters. Financing charges and interest rates are high—sometimes as much as 18 per cent. The lower-priced mobiles are often too small, too fragile, too hot in summer, and too cold in winter. Many units are relegated to run-down neighborhoods by ordinance and zoning laws and still others are located in parks, which due to lack of community regulations or fast buck developers, or both leaves the occupying family in a depressing environment.

Renting Mobiles

Mobile homes are not confined to urban areas but represent as much as 15 per cent of the rural housing in some states with the percentage in most states not this high but steadily climbing. Many small real estate investors are making a good return on capital by renting mobiles and there is a definite upward trend in this business.

Whether this would be a good investment for you depends to a great extent on how much time you are prepared to spend, not only in renting your units, maintenance and collecting rents, but in shopping for good rental unit buys. Many rental units are acquired as used units and often are repossessions acquired from banks and/or mobile home dealers.

Selling Land for Mobile Homes

Recently I sold 25 acres of land close to Charleston, West Virginia to a mobile home dealer who plans to develop the property into a park for rental units, using his own repossessions and others he can pick up from local banks at bargain prices. He contemplates rental income of from $125 to $150 monthly and will likely acquire most of the units in the $2,000 to $4,000 price range. On the surface this sounds like a terrific investment with perhaps a three to five year pay out. It may well be, on the otherhand, that vacancies plus depreciation through deterioration by wearing out and abuse and/or obsolescence will considerably reduce his profits. Then too, he will have a considerable outlay of capital in purchasing and developing his land.

Financing Mobile Units

Most mobile home financing is usually arranged by the dealer who sells the unit. Banks, savings and loan associations, credit unions, and finance companies make mobile home loans.

There are Government-backed programs that assist in financing, and there are conventional loans.

In a conventional loan, a down payment of 20 per cent to 30 per cent is usually required. Repayment time can be as long as 10 years. The average term is from five to seven years. Interest ranges from 11 per cent to 15 per cent and is usually computed by an add-on method. By this method, the interest is added to the principal amount (net proceeds) of the loan when it is made and the interest cost remains the same over the entire term of the loan.

HUD's mobile home financing is provided under Title I of the National Housing Act. Under this program, banks and other financial institutions pay HUD an insurance program of 50 cents per $100 per year of net advance and are insured for 90 per cent of the loss.

To qualify for a HUD-insured mobile home loan, the borrower must have sufficient funds to make a specified small down payment and sufficient income to make payments on the loan; he must intend to use the mobile home as his principal residence; and he must have an acceptable site on which the mobile home is to be placed. Such a site may be rented space in a mobile home park, or it may be on his own land. The site must meet HUD standards, and there must be no violation of zoning requirements or other regulations applicable to mobile homes.

The mobile home must be at least 10 feet wide and 40 feet long, and meet HUD construction standards for mobile homes; it must be new or, if not new, it must have been financed with a HUD-insured loan when it was new and the total price of the mobile home may include furnishings, appliances, and accessory items as well as transportation to the site where it will be occupied and the initial premium for mobile home insurance.

The maximum loan is $10,000 for a single unit and $15,000 for a double-wide. Maximum term is 12 years for single unit and 15 years for larger units. Interest percentage varies from 7.63 per cent to 10.57 per cent, depending on the amount and term of the loan.

Five per cent of the total price is required for down payment on a unit costing up to $6,000 and 10 per cent on any portion of the cost over $6,000. Loans are secured by conditional sales contracts on chattel mortgages on the unit and the lender pays ½ of 1 per cent per annum of loan proceeds for HUD insurance premium.

MOBILE HOME PARKS

When you think of mobile home parks your reflections will likely be influenced by where you live or places you have visited.

If your community has refused to zone and grant permits for parks, and in effect has relegated them to outlying areas where the developer is completely unregulated, or through improper zoning has limited them to run down or industrial areas—you may look on them as unwelcome and undesirable neighbors.

On the other hand, if you are from Florida or the Southwest, where most ma and pa trailer camp type operations have been replaced by planned developments with wide curbed and guttered paved streets and offering all the amenities anticipated in a middle to upper income apartment complex; you likely have a more benevolent opinion of the mobile park. Swimming pools, club houses, sauna baths, and affiliation with nearby golf courses are not unique in modern parks.

What Size Park?

Arriving at the proper size of a mobile home park presents about the same problem as the same decision pertaining to an apartment complex.

I have seen many semi-retired couples use an extra lot next to their home for from five to 15 units and in most instances it was a satisfactory, profitable arrangement.

Generally speaking, the park should be small enough to permit you to manage it within the budget of your time or large enough to operate economically with a full-time manager. Where outside management is hired, most owners feel that 75 to 100 spaces is minimum and larger parks with 150 or more spaces work better.

Density and Income

Acceptable densities of units per acre varies with terrain and land costs. While many of the older parks have 15 or 20 or more units per acre crowded within their boundaries, the trend seems to be six to eight units per acre leaving ample room for parking, landscaping, swimming pool, shuffleboard court, tot lots, and other amenities.

Spaces may rent from $25 a month on the low side to $100 and more on the high side. The park owner/developer often includes water and sewer charges in the base rent with the tenant paying fuel bills. Coin-operated laundry and other vending machines are additional income sources in larger parks.

Financing Mobile Parks

Financing for mobile home parks may be from commercial banks, savings and loans, syndicates or institutional investors. Most lenders, however, still take a conservative approach–restricting loans to around 50 per cent of the value and amortization to 10 to 12 years.

Recognizing the need for raising the standards of new parks and upgrading existing ones, Congress in 1969 amended an older housing law in an effort to make it easier for private developers to finance sites for mobile home parks.

HUD Insured Loans

Under the current HUD program the maximum insurable loan may equal the lesser of:

1. $1 million ($1,450,000 in high-cost areas).
2. Ninety (90) per cent of HUD's estimated value of the park site after completion of improvements, assuming the land is held in fee simple.
3. $2,500 per home space ($3,625 in high-cost areas).

Mortgage terms may be up to 40 years but not appreciably in excess of three-fourths of the estimated remaining economic life of the project. Also 90 per cent of the park's estimated net income must be sufficient to meet the mortgage requirements.

Interest rate will be the HUD rate, in effect, when mortgage is insured and borrower pays ½ of 1 per cent mortgage insurance premium.

Leased land may be used but leasehold must be at least 75 years. One automobile parking space is required for each home space and the park must contain such public utilities and neighborhood amenities necessary to make the property permanently attractive, in comparison with other residential developments in the community.

Good Parks Are Still Needed

Although mobile home parks have increased, both in size and total numbers, in recent years most markets do not appear in immediate danger of saturation. Most mobile home dealers consider the lack of adequate park facilities to be their single greatest drawback to sales and in many communities dealers have been forced into park development to keep their sales from bogging down due to lack of available spaces.

25

RECREATION LAND

Workers today have more leisure time than those of yesterday and the probability is great that the next generation will work less hours than this one.

In 1850 the average work week was 70 hours. Today it is less than 40 hours and many predict 30 hours or less will be standard by the year 2000. In addition to a shorter work week, the numbers of retired and semi-retired persons are rising; youth works less and has more leisure time than earlier generations; average years of schooling has been extended; and modern equipment in the homes has given the housewife more free time.

Despite a much wider distribution of income than ever before, our country is one of economic contrasts. While millions of Americans in 1972 had incomes below the nationally pegged poverty level, others spent more and more on the good life. Some estimate the leisure time market accounts for a total annual expenditure of 100 billion dollars–more than the cost of national defense.

Although these figures are perhaps more exciting to travel bureaus and sports equipment manufacturers than to land speculators, a sizable expenditure is required for land and related improvements. For example, production in travel trailers rose from 62,600 in 1961 to 549,000 in 1972, which means that a lot of additional land is required each year for travel trailer parks.

While ski industry revenues to land developers undoubtedly lag behind that of orthopedic surgeons who repaired some 50,000 broken legs in the 1972 season, the 1,200 developed ski resorts represent sizable real estate investments.

With nearly 11,000 courses in the country, golf is still growing and tennis and boating are booming. Other booming recreational industries such as snowmobiling, bicycling, motorcycling, and so forth may not require new land acquisitions *per se* but undoubtedly mean more second homes or weekend cottages. There are now three million two-home families and their number is growing at the rate of 200,000 per year.

The recreation potential of farmland, now in great demand by city dwellers, may not be the primary motivation for purchasing in most instances but it usually plays a significant part. Some land is, of course, acquired solely for recreation such as hunting and fishing, but buyers who are looking for farm or mountain acreage for cottages or second homes often prefer that it be located near a ski lodge, golf course, fishing lake, and so forth.

Many large subdivisions are now developed around recreational facilities such as golf courses and fishing lakes. Most developers are not interested in the long range profit potential of these facilities but count on taking their money on the front end in the form of increased residential lot prices.

Depending upon where you live, the opportunities for selling real estate for recreation purposes may be great or almost nil.

26

INDUSTRIALIZED HOUSING

A few years back, many people were predicting factory produced modular housing would soon dominate the residential housing field—particularly on the lower end of the scale.

George Romney, Secretary of HUD said in 1971: "I predict that by the end of this decade, at least two-thirds of all housing production in the United States will be factory produced."

Major Types

There are two major types of industrialized housing:

1. Modulars. Three dimensional units—usually trucked to the job site in two sections and joined together on the preinstalled foundation. These are most commonly used for single family housing but are sometimes stacked to create multifamily buildings.
2. Panelized Housing. Roof trusses, walls, ceiling and floor sections are constructed in a central factory (or sometimes a factory built on the site for a large development). Where built in a central factory, the manufacturer usually supplies windows, doors, molding, lighting, plumbing and electrical fixtures—everything to complete the house with the exception of the foundation and landscaping.

Failures Many—Growth Slow

Many rushed into this business undercapitalized. Some started with ample capital, but little know-how. The failures have been numerous. Divisions of ITT and Frauhauf have been among the dropouts. A leading national homebuilder's magazine reported that 50 new companies entered the field in 1972 and 90 bowed out.

The production of modulars almost doubled in 1971 over 1970, but 1972 indicated roughly a 5 per cent increase over the previous years—a year in which housing starts registered a 15 per cent gain over the preceding 12-month period. About one-third of the companies in this business are publicly held and little more than two-thirds of their units go into single family homes. Quality control, damage in shipping, lack of uniformity in building codes, and in some instances lack of public acceptance have been the big drawbacks. Some manufacturers who entered the business on the strength of HUD programs (Section 235 and Section 236) may encounter difficulties as the result of moratoriums placed on subsidized housing in early 1973.

Optimism and Drawbacks

While in their best years, modular housing manufacturers have supplied less than 3 per cent of the nation's total housing, many developers still see this type of housing as a major influence in the future.

Panelized housing has less problems, particularly in shipping, than modular housing. The chief drawback to this business has been the failure of the manufacturers to price the units at a savings to developers over stick building, in many areas.

Developers, generally, have had their greatest battle in trying to hold down the price of land and financing—regardless of which construction approach is used.

Part III

Heavy Hand in Housing—Government Programs

27

HUD–HISTORY AND PROGRAMS

No land speculator can consider his knowledge adequate without some understanding of The Department of Housing and Urban Development (HUD).

Established in 1965, it is composed of numerous Federal agencies, some dating back to the 1930's. Best known of these agencies is the Federal Housing Administration (FHA) established in 1934. The Public Housing Administration (PHA) followed in 1937. The Urban Renewal Administration (URA) was created in 1949. HUD's predecessor was the Housing and Home Finance Agency (HHFA), acting somewhat as a coordinator of these programs. Even after the passage of the 1965 HUD act, the various agencies continued to function in a quasi-independent manner. FHA retained its name; PHA became the Housing Assistance Administration (HAA); and URA became the Renewal Assistance Administration (RAA).

Secretary George Romney announced a new HUD structure in 1969 in an effort to achieve coordination and better control over the various agencies. A follow-up internal reorganization was instituted in early 1971 and reshuffling continues. Many builders, developers, and even many HUD employees question whether the new organization is as efficient as were the various organizations acting independently or in a loose confederacy.

Initially, and for many years, FHA was concerned mainly with the Section 203 program, whereby, for an insurance premium of 0.5 per cent paid by the borrower, the lender was insured against the borrower's default. No subsidy is involved in this program and millions of families have been able to achieve home ownership where otherwise it would not have been possible or at least they would have been forced to delay buying a home for many years until they accumulated a large equity payment.

HUD Insured Programs

HUD/FHA presently insures numerous other programs in a similar fashion as follows:

Title I: Home Improvements and Mobile Homes
Section 207: Multi-Family and Mobile Home Parks
Section 213: Cooperatives
Section 220: Homes and Multi-Family in Urban Renewal Areas
Section 221: Homes and Multi-Family for Moderate-Income and Displaced Families
Section 222: Mortgage Insurance of Homes for Servicemen
Section 231: Mortgage Insurance of Rental Housing for the Elderly
Section 232: Intermediate Care Facilities and Nursing Homes
Section 233: Experimental Housing Projects
Section 234: Condominiums
Section 240: Insurance for Purchase of Fee-Simple Title
Section 241: Supplemental Loan Insurance for Multi-Family Housing
Section 242: Mortgage Insurance for Non-Profit Hospitals
Title X: Mortgage Insurance for Land Development
Title XI: Mortgage Insurance for Group Practice Facilities

The above programs involve only insurance and not assistance or subsidy. Subsidized housing is discussed more fully in another section.

Other HUD Programs

HUD is also responsible for numerous other programs including low interest rate direct loans for college housing programs and subsidization of interest rates on private loans for this purpose. Community development programs include Urban Renewal, model cities, water and sewer systems, neighborhood facilities, open space lands, and public facilities. HUD, like most federal governmental agencies, prints considerable literature on its programs, most of which is available for the asking at any regional office.

HUD's Influence on Raw Land

The price of undeveloped property is often influenced greatly by HUD's willingness to insure loans on housing to be constructed on the land. In both buying and selling unimproved residential property you should take this into consideration. In selling unimproved land to a developer, you may be able to get a much better price by securing HUD's preliminary approval based on a survey, topo map, and an engineer's lay-out of your subdivision on a map.

In dealing in improved residential property, the amount of the required down payment and the required monthly payments have a great influence on your ability to sell. Both the property and the purchaser must be acceptable to obtain HUD insurance. Being familiar with the agency's requirements may increase your sales and your profits. Like all Federal governmental agencies; the rules, regulations, policies, and red tape are a little frightening. Only a very few of the agency's programs will, however, have a direct effect on the values of property you buy and sell. I suggest you keep current on the Section 203 program, subsidy programs for single and multifamily housing, and subdivision regulations governing your area. In addition to information available through your regional HUD office, local developers, real estate agencies, loan correspondents for mortgage bankers, and HUD approved mortgages are all good sources of information on HUD programs.

MULTIFAMILY SUBSIDY PROGRAMS

The first Federal venture into subsidized multifamily housing was accomplished under Section 221 (d)(3)–Below Market Interest Rate (BMIR) program, which was enacted into law by congress in 1961. This Section made available 3 per cent interest rate loans to limited dividend partnerships and non-profit owners. The owners were required to pass the advantage of the low interest rates on to low and moderate income tenants in the form of reduced rents.

Section 236 Program

This program was largely phased out in recent years and succeeded by Section 236 of the Housing and Urban Development Act of 1968. The purpose of this program is to provide rental housing for low and moderate income families or individuals 62 years or older or handicapped—with occupancy priority going to individuals or families displaced by urban renewal or other governmental actions.

Under this program, private mortgage loans are insured and a portion of the interest charged for such loans is subsidized. Interest subsidy is accomplished by making monthly payments to the mortgagee to reduce the owner's payment below the market rate. Benefits from subsidized interest rates are passed on to tenants in the form of lower rents.

Many 236 programs have been developed by non-profit groups. The limited-dividend partnership approach has, however, been more successful. Benefits to owners under this program are discussed under the Chapter on "Tax Shelters."

Numerous Failures

Recently, these subsidy programs have had numerous failures and have come under heavy criticism. Some have worked beautifully toward achieving the purpose for which the program was designed. Other projects have failed miserably because they were ill-conceived, poorly built, or poorly managed. In some areas both developers and HUD officials have come under heavy criticism and some have been convicted for fraud in the form of kick-backs, favors, and misrepresentations, and so forth.

In the event you have land you believe to be suitable for a 236 project, you should contact a reliable developer in this business or the HUD insuring office with jurisdiction in your area. Individual programs will come and go but the Federal Government through HUD or a successor agency will continue in the housing business. The more you know about current HUD programs, the better your chances for selling land for insured and/or subsidized housing.

PUBLIC HOUSING FOR THE LOW INCOME

The public housing program dates back to the United States Housing Acts of 1937. This program is Federally financed and locally operated, usually by five-person boards or commissions appointed by the mayor or the local governing body, and serving without compensation. The Board, referred to as the local housing authority (LHA), employs a paid executive director and such other staff as necessary—depending on the scope of the program.

There are about 3,000 such housing authorities throughout the United States and Puerto Rico. Public housing units are exempt from local real estate taxes but the act permits payment in lieu of taxes to the local community in an amount equal to 10 per cent of gross rent less utilities. Before HUD will approve a local program an LHA must enter into a *cooperation agreement* with the city, whereby the city agrees to provide the usual municipal services to the proposed housing project.

Who Qualifies for Public Housing?

Occupants of public housing units range from welfare families to families with incomes of up to five or six thousand dollars annually—depending on the area and size of the family. Rent to be charged is left up to LHA, subject to local review and the statutory requirement that no tenant can pay more than one-fourth of his income as rent.

How Projects Are Developed

An LHA may construct or acquire its public housing units. When it does its own construction—this is referred to as the "conventional" method, and when it acquired its new or rehabilitated units ready for occupancy by a builder or developer—this is referred to as the "turnkey" method.

Providing Housing Sites

Public housing has two major categories:

1. Family housing
2. Elderly housing

Since, as a speculator in land your main interest would be in providing the land, you should become acquainted with the executive director of the LHA in your area to determine whether new projects are contemplated and what the site requirements will be.

Most often in larger cities where land is scarce and expensive, elderly housing is provided through "hi-rise" buildings. In smaller areas it is often single story apartments. Family housing is usually two-story apartments or row houses and requires more land area to meet the need for playgrounds for the children.

Where housing is constructed under the conventional method you would deal directly with the LHA. If turnkey method is used, the land would be acquired by a private developer who has contracted to sell a completed project to the LHA.

While certain guidelines are established governing site selection and price, the Federal regulations are very complex and change from time to time. Your only reliable source of information is the executive director of the LHA contemplating a project.

Based on my experience with some $30 million dollars worth of projects in turnkey public housing, I have acquired raw land at prices varying from approximately $500 to approximately $2,000 per apartment unit for both family and elderly housing. Projects have been constructed in other parts of the country on cheaper land and on more expensive land.

Density of units will depend upon local codes and HUD regulations. For elderly hi-rise, about one acre is required for 100 units in a ten story building. A taller building will, of course, require less land and a lower one more land. Family apartment density will vary from about five units per acre to 20 or more an acre–depending on the availability and price of land.

Leased Housing

For many years the LHA owned all of its public housing units. In 1965, however, Congress provided the right to lease units from private owners and in turn sublease these to low-income tenants. This program is commonly referred to as *leased housing*, or "Section 23 housing"–derived from its section number in the United States Housing Act.

Where a project is owned by an LHA (either conventionally or turnkey developed) it is financed through the issuance of 40-year, tax exempt bonds–with HUD pledging to contribute each year's payment of principal and interest on these bonds.

Under the leased housing program the LHA pays the landlord from tenant rents and HUD annual contributions or subsidies.

From leased payments from the LHA, the owner pays his debt service, taxes, and costs of exterior maintenance; provides reserves; and attempts to achieve a satisfactory cash flow.

The builder/developer may own the project and receive tax shelter benefits or in order to get a better interest rate, he may work with the LHA to establish a non-profit corporation to actually own the project and make his profit from "front-end" construction contract.

From the standpoint of the land speculator, however, the opportunity for sale of property to a developer is essentially the same as where ownerships of the project is acquired by the LHA from a developer who builds under a "turnkey" contract.

FINANCING HUD INSURED AND SUBSIDIZED HOUSING

Developers may seek a loan on HUD insured and subsidized housing through approved lenders. Generally, lending institutions which have a net worth of more than $100,000 and otherwise qualify may be approved by HUD. Most commercial banks and savings and loan associations are approved lenders. Mortgage banks usually deal heavily in these loans.

The Federal National Mortgage Association

The Federal National Mortgage Association (Fannie Mae) was chartered in 1938 as a subsidiary of The Reconstruction Finance Corporation. Supervision of this agency was transferred to the Housing and Home Finance Agency in 1950.

The Agency was reorganized in 1954, and in 1968 it was divided into two separate and distinct corporations–one known as the Government National Mortgage Association (GNMA or Ginnie Mae) which retained certain functions previously delegated to

FNMA, which agency now became a Federal government regulated but privately owned corporation.

Borrowing money on the open market, Fannie Mae uses these funds to trade mainly in government-insured mortgages, although it is legally permitted to deal in conventional mortgages.

Through frequent auctions, it makes funds available for commitments to purchase HUD and VA insured single family mortgages. Sellers bid for three-month commitments covering existing structures and 12-month commitments covering new construction.

This is commonly referred to as the secondary mortgage market and the results of the auctions appear in the Wall Street Journal—providing developers and mortgage sellers with current price information.

The Government National Mortgage Association

Ginnie Mae is a wholly government owned corporation. Its sources of revenue include sale of participation certificates to private investors, portfolio liquidation, net earnings, and borrowing from the United States Treasury.

Ginnie Mae provides special assistance for financing subsidized mortgages, manages and liquidates the government's portfolio of mortgages, pools government backed mortgages, sells participations in these securities to private interests, and guarantees debt securities issued by Fannie Mae or other government approved lenders.

The Federal Home Loan Bank Board

The Federal Home Loan Bank (FHLBB) was created in 1932 as an independent Federal agency governed by a three-member Board. It sets policies, establishes regulations, and supervises the operations of The Federal Home Loan Bank System, the Federal Savings and Loan Insurance Corporation, The Federal Savings and Loan System, and oversees the operations of The Federal Home Loan Mortgage Corporation.

Federal Home Loan Mortgage Corporation

Created in 1970 (FHLMC) was vested by Congress with the authority to establish a secondary market in residential mortgages. It buys single and multifamily residential loans from sellers who have deposits insured by an agency of the Federal Government and which are members of the Federal Home Loan Bank System.

INDEX

Absolute auction, 146
Absorption of land, 26
Abstract of title, 110-111
Acquisition and ownership, 108-119
abstract of title, 110-111
certificate of title, 111
closing statement, 113-114
deed, 112
escrow, 112
fee simple title, 112
insuring investment, 117-119
listing, 108-109
offer to purchase, 109-110
recording deed, 114
records essential, 116-117
survey, 111
title, taking, 114-116
corporation, 116
dower and curtsey, 115
joint tenancy, 116
limited partnerships or syndicates, 116
partnership, 116
tenancy in common, 115-116
tenancy by entirety, 115
trusts, 116
title insurance, 111
title search, 110
trust deed, 112-113
Advertising, 173-174
Advice, when to take, 44
Aerial survey, using for subdivision, 89-90
Agricultural agents, getting to know, 38
Agricultural Extension Service, 135
Agricultural property, beginning with, 34
Agricultural Stabilization and Conservation Service, 136
American Land Development Association, 23
Analyzing and forecasting, 120-132
cycles, 121
economy, growing, 126-127
and emotional influences, 127-128
Depression, 127-128 (see also "Depression")
employment trends, 122
Federal Reserve System, 122
indicators, other, 122-123
inflation, growth and, 125-126
land booms, other, 132
in small communities, 123-124
supply and demand, law of, 123
uniqueness of each situation, 124
Annexation laws, knowledge of as necessary tool, 36-37
Apartment business less affected by national patterns, 123-124
Apartments, condominiums and cooperatives, 182-190
condominiums and cooperatives, 186-189

Apartments (cont.)
advantages, 187-188
compared, 187
condominiums most popular, 188
financing, 188-189
HUD insured financing, 189-190
duplex or fourplex, 183
expense/income ratio, 184
financing, 169-172, 186
increased number of, reasons for, 182-183
land, supplying, 184-185
size, 183-184
"swinging singles," 185-186
Appraising for speculation, 164-168
approaches, three, 165-166
land areas, computing, 167-168
land measurement table, 168
Argonaut Realty Company, 66
ASCS, 136
Assessment in area, knowledge of as necessary tool, 35-36
Astor, John Jacob, 8
Attorney, when to take advice of, 44
Auctions, buying and selling at, 144-148
bidding, beginning of, 146-148
bi-bidding, 147
how to buy at, 146
importance of attending, 37
property for, suitable, 145-146
types of, 146

B

Bank for Cooperatives, 141
Bankers, when to take advice of, 44
Banks, commercial, financing from, 169-170
Bargain situations, buying into, 65-68
Barton, Bruce, 33
Beginning, 32-45
goals, setting, 39-41
liquidity, importance of preserving, 41, 44-45
value, factors influencing, 40-41
Beginning (cont.)
judgment, using your own, 41-45
advice, when to take, 44
questions, qualifying, 32-33
things to know, 33-34
brokers, help from, 34
familiar surroundings essential, 33-34
fundamentals, 38-39
tools to use, 35-38
undeveloped property, 34
Below Market Interest Rate program of 1961, 214
Bernstein, George K., 106
Bi-bidding, 147
Bidding at auction, beginning of, 146-148
bi-bidding, 147
Binder agreement, 109-110
Birthrate, declining, importance of, 27-28
Blind pool offerings in public syndication, 158-159
BMIR program of 1961, 214
Bounds, use of in identification of property in survey, 99-100
Brokerage, 175-178
commissions, 176
licensing laws, 175-176
multiple listings, 177
net listings and open listings, 177
pros and cons of, 177-178
and speculation not compatible, 178
Brokers, help from, 34
signs of, exploring, 37
Bush-hog, use of, 40

C

Capitalization approach to appraising, 166
Carnegie, Andrew, 48
Cash, available, essential for dealing in cheap property, 71
Caveat emptor, 97-107
mail order land buying, 101-107
Florida, paradox of, 105-106
HUD, experience of, 106-107
laws tightened, 103-104
misrepresentation and overpricing, 103

Caveat Emptor *(cont.)*
questions for consideration, 97-99
recreational or retirement developments, 105-106
surveying, 99-101
deed, plotting, 101
expenses of, 100-101
identification, proper, 99-100
Central Bank for Cooperatives, 141
Cheap property, 70-71
Choices of what to buy, making profitable, 72-74
Chrysler Realty Company, 23
Closing statement, 113-114
Commercial banks, financing from, 37, 169-170
Commissions of broker, 176
Common stocks, real estate versus, 46-51
real estate, advantages of, 47-48
disadvantages of owning, 50
stocks, advantages and disadvantages of, 49-51
Community factors, local, affecting real estate sales, 123
Comparable sales approach to appraising, 165-166
Compensation to expect, 56-59
Condominiums, 182-190 (see also "Apartments . . . . . .")
Coolidge, Calvin, 130
Cooperative Farm Credit System, 141-142
Cooperatives, 182-190 (see also "Apartments . . . . . .")
Corporation ownership, 116
Corporations, large, investments of in real estate, 23
Cost of land a factor in subdividing residential land, 87-88
Covenants, suggested protective for subdivisions, 92-94
Credit, using to increase returns, 56
Curtsey, 115
Cycles, 121

D

DDB, 155
Declining balance method of calculating depreciation, 151
Deed, 112
plotting, 101
recording, 114
Depreciation, 149-157
calculating, 150
declining balance method, 151
economic obsolescence, 149-150
and IRS guidelines, current, 154-155
of residential property, 154
schedule, 155-157
straight-line method, 150-151
sum-of-the-digits method, 151-152
Depression, effect of, 127-128
conditions preceding, 128
Florida land boom, 128-132
Developers, 162-163
selling to, 69-70
Distress property, 71-72
leveraging on, 72
Distress sales, buying at, 144-148 (see also "Auctions . . . .")
Doubled price in three or four years, criterion of, 54
Dower, 115
Duplex, 183

E

Earnest money receipt, 109-110
Economic obsolescence, 149-150
Economic Research Service, 137, 142*n*
Economy, growing, real estate and, 126-127
Elderly housing, providing sites for, 216-217
Emotional influences, real estate and, 127-128
Employment trends as influencing factor, 122
Environment, protecting, in subdividing, 94-95
Escrow, 112
Expansion in area, benefitting from, 55-56

F

Familiar surroundings essential at beginning, 33-34

Family housing for low incomes, sites for, 216-217
Fannie Mae, 218-219
"Farm Index," 136-137
Farm property, buying and selling, 133-143
  Agricultural Extension Service, 135
  Agricultural Stabilization and Conservation Service, 136
  considerations, 137-139
  financing, 139-142
    Farmers Home Administration, 139-141
    Federal Land Bank, 141
    Production Credit Associations, 141-142
  for investment, 134-135
  knowledge of farming important, 134
  quick profit on, 133
  no shortages, 136-137
  Soil Conservation Service, 135-136
  value per acre of farm real estate, change in regional, 142
  Vo-Ag teachers, using, 135
Farmers Home Administration, 53, 139-141
Farmland, choice of to buy, 73
  rising prices of, 22, 29-30
Federal Home Loan Bank, 219
Federal Home Loan Mortgage Corp., 220
Federal Land Bank, 141
Federal National Mortgage Association, 218-219
Federal Reserve System as influencing factor, 122
Fee simple title, 112
Financing, 169-172
  commercial banks, 169-170
  individual lenders, 172
  knowledge of as necessary tool, 37
  life insurance companies, 171
  mortgage companies, 171-172
  savings and loan associations, 170
Financing farmland, 139-142 (see also "Farm property . . . .")
Florida, paradox of, 105-106
  land boom of, Depression and, 128-132
FmHA, 139-141
Ford Motor Company, 23
Forecasting, 120-132 (see also "Analyzing and forecasting")
Foreclosure sales, 144-148 (see also "Auctions . . . . . .")
Foreign lands, rising land prices in, 24
Fourplex, 183
Four-year plan of turning over property, 59-63
Franklin, Benjamin, 43
Frauhauf, 210

G

General Motors, 66
Ginnie Mae, 218-219
Goals, setting, 39-41
Government National Mortgage Association, 218-219
Government programs, 211-220
  HUD—history and programs, 212-220
Growth of area, effect of on value, 40, 55-56
Growth regions, change in, 31

H

Hampton Institute, 200
Holding land, expense of, 24-25
Home ownership, 74-80
  advantages, 75-76
  disadvantages, 76-80
  mortgage, how to gain on, 79-80
Home sites, rising prices of, 23
Homeowner's policy, 119
Hoover, Herbert, 130
Housing, industrialized, 209-210
  drawbacks, 210
  growth slow, 209-210
  optimism, 210
  types, two, 209
Housing Acts of 1937, 216
Housing programs, low and moderate income, structuring of as most favorable tax shelter, 154

Housing and Urban Development Act of 1968, 215
HUD–history and programs, 212-220
background of, 212-213
experience of with mail order land buying, 106-107
financing, 218-220
construction of housing projects, 189-190
Federal Home Loan Bank, 219
Federal Home Loan Mortgage Corp., 220
Federal National Mortgage Association, 218-219
Government National Mortgage Association, 218-219
for mobile home parks, 206
leased housing, 217-218
low income housing, 216-218
development of projects, 216-217
sites, providing, 216-217
who qualifies, 216
mortgagee, qualifications for, 172
programs currently insured, 213-214
raw land, its influence on, 214
subsidy programs, multifamily, 214-215
BMIR of 1961, 214
failures, 215
Section 236 program, 215

I

Identification, proper, of land to be surveyed, 99-100
Improvements to property, effect of on value, 40, 52-53
Income, doubling, 56-59
Income, need for as reason for owner's desire to sell in future, 83
Individual lenders as source of financing, 37, 172
Industrial property, rising prices of, 23
Industrial real estate, 193-199
industrial parks, 197-199
Industrial real estate (*cont.*)
price of land, 198-199
warehousing, 194-196
speculative buildings, 194-196
Industrialized housing, 209-210 (see also "Housing, industrialized")
Inflation, effect of on value, 40
condominiums and cooperatives as hedge against, 187
growth and, 125-126
Insurance companies as source of financing, 171
Insurance for your investment, 117-119
Investment in farmland, 134-135
Investment trusts, 159-160
Investor, meaning of, 9-11
Investor's reasons for buying, 65
IRS guidelines, current, for depreciation and tax shelters, 154-155
ITT, 210

J

J.C. Penney's, 192
Joint tenancy, 116
Joint venture, 160-162 (see also "Syndicating real estate")
Journal of Forestry, 95
Judgment, using your own, 41-45

K

Knowledge of farming important to deal in farmland, 134

L

Land boom, greatest, 21-25
competition from large corporations, 23
farmland, rising prices of, 22
in foreign lands, 24
holding land, expense of, 24-25
home sites, 23
industrial property, 23
multifamily housing, 23-24
prices, rising, 21-22
second homes, 23
Land measurement table, 168
Landlord's profit, elimination of in condominium and cooperative, 187-188

Leased housing, 217-218
Leopold, Aldo, 95
Leverage, 81-85
  on distressed property, 72
  to increase returns, using, 56
  interest, none, 84-85
  methods to obtain, two, 81
  option possibilities, 85
  possibilities for in subdividing residential property, 89
  real estate, greatest opportunities in, 84
  reserves in time and money, keeping, 85
  risk, 83
  tax shelters and, 152-154
LHA, 216
Licensing laws, 175-176
Life insurance companies as source of financing, 171
Limited partnerships or syndicates, 116
Liquidity, importance of preserving, 41, 44-45
Listing, 108-109, 177
Litton Industries, 84
Lot and block number identification of land in survey, 99
Low income housing, 216-218
  development of projects, 216-217
  sites, providing, 216-217
  who qualifies, 216

M

McMichael, Stanley L., 168
McMichael's Appraising Manual, 168
Mail order land buying, 101-107
  Florida, paradox of, 105-106
  HUD, experience of, 106-107
  laws tightened, 103-104
  misrepresented and overpriced, 103
Malone, Walter, 58*n*
Maps as necessary tool, 35
Mellon, Andrew, 131
Metes and bounds as property identification in survey, 99-100
Miami Herald, 22, 105
Misrepresentation in mail order land buying, 103
Mobile homes, 200-206
  disadvantages, 202
  financing, 203-204
  land for, selling, 203
  luxury, trend toward, 202
  parks, 204-206
    density and income, 205
    financing, 205-206
    HUD insured loans, 206
    size of, 205
  reasons for, 201
  renting, 202-203
  where most used, 201
  who uses, 201
Modular housing, 209-210
Monuments as identification term in property to be surveyed, 100
Mortgage companies as source of financing, 37, 171-172
Mortgage for your home, how to gain on, 79-80
Multifamily housing, 23-24
Multiple listings, 177
Mutual insurance companies, 117

N

National banks, financing from, 169-170
National Housing Act, 154
Net listings, 177
New York Life Insurance Company, 171
Newspaper advertisements as source of information, 38
North, Nelson L., 78

O

Offer to purchase, 109-110
Open listings, 177
Opinion Research Corporation, 30-31
Opportunity, recognizing, 68
Option possibilities, 85
Overdeveloping, avoiding, 90
Overpricing in mail order land buying, 103
Ownership, 108-119 (see also "Acquisition and ownership")

Ownership of land in U.S., major categories of, 27

P

Packagers of real estate, 162-163
Panelized housing, 209-210
Parks, industrial, 197-199
Partnership type of ownership, 116
PCA's, 141-142
People, land and, 26-31
 absorption of land, 26
 birthrate, declining, 27-28
 densities of population, future and, 27
 ownership of land in U.S., major categories of, 27
 shifts in land use, 28
 trends, 28-31
  farmland prices high, 29-30
  growth regions, change in, 31
  where people want to live, 30-31
Population densities, future and, 27
Population trends, 28-31
 farmland prices high, 29-30
 growth regions, change in, 31
 where people want to live, 30-31
Positive self-image, need for, 58
Prices of land, rising, 21-22
Production Credit Associations, 141-142
Profit goal, how to reach, 21-178 (see also under particular heading)
 acquisition and ownership, 108-119
 advertising, 173-174
 analyzing and forecasting, 120-132
 appraising for speculation, 164-168
 auction, buying and selling at, 144-148
 beginning, 32-45
 brokerage, 175-178
 caveat emptor, 97-107
 common stocks, real estate versus, 46-51
 depreciation and tax shelters, 149-152
Profit goal *(cont.)*
 farm property, buying and selling, 133-143
 financing, 169-172
 land boom, greatest, 21-25
 leverage, 81-85
 people, land and, 26-31
 raw land and, 52-63
 subdividing residential land, 86-96
 syndicating real estate, 158-163
 tax shelters, 152-157
 what to buy, 64-80
Project development, 216-217
 types of, two, 216
Promoters, 162-163
Property taxes, knowledge of as necessary tool, 35-36
Public housing for low income, 216-218
 development of projects, 216-217
 housing sites, providing, 216-217
 who qualifies, 216
Public syndication, 158-159
Purchase offer, 109-110

Q

Quality of land important to apartment builder, 184-185
Questions, qualifying, for real estate trading career, 32-33
Questions for consideration by buyer, 97-99

R

Raw land, HUD's influence on, 214
Raw land and profits, 52-63
 compensation to expect, 56-59
  four-year plan, 59-63
 credit, using to increase returns, 56
 how much, 54-56
  doubled price in three or four years, criterion of, 54
  10%, adding by beautifying, 55
  20% below average market price, buying at, 54
 improved property, 52-53

Raw land and profits *(cont.)*
leveraging, 56
positive self-image, need for, 58
statistics, 53
Raw property, beginning with, 34
Real Estate Principles and Practices, 78
Reason for buying, 65
Recording deed, 114
Records essential, 116-117
Recreation land, 207-208
Recreational developments, speculating in, 105-106
Rectangular survey, 100
Reproduction costs approach to appraising, 166
Reserves, keeping adequate, 85
Residences, single-family, 180-181
Residential land, subdividing, 86-96 (see also "Subdividing residential land")
Residential lots, buying, 73
Residential property, depreciation of, 154
Retirement developments, speculating in, 105-106
Ring, Alfred A., 78
Risk great with leverage, 83
Rogers, Will, 24
Romney, George, 209, 212
Roosevelt, Theodore, 64

S

Sales contract, 109-110
Savings and loan associations as source of financing, 37, 170
SCS, 38, 135-136
Sears Roebuck Co., 192
Second homes, rising price of, 23
Secondary mortgage market, 219
Secular trends, cycle of, 121
Self-image, need for positive, 58
Shifting, constant, of real estate, 64
Shifts in use of lands, 28
Shopping centers, 191-192
Shortages nonexistent in farmland, 136-137
Single-family residences, 180-181
Sleepers, buying, 65-68
Small communities less influenced by national patterns, 123-124
Smith, Adam, 52
Smith, Al, 130-131
Soil Conservation Service, 135-136
getting to know agents of, 38
Sources of financing, 169-172 (see also "Financing")
Specific property offerings in public syndication, 158-159
Speculation and brokerage not compatible, 178
Speculator, definition of, 9-10
Speculator's reasons for buying, 65
Statistics, real estate, 53
Stock insurance companies, 117-118
Stocks, advantages and disadvantages of owning, 49-51
Stocks, common, 46-51 (see also "Common stocks, real estate versus")
Straight line method of calculating depreciation, 150-151
Sub Chapter S Corporation, designation of joint venture as, 161
Subdividing residential land, 86-96
covenants, protective, 91-94
demand, reasons for, 86-87
do's and don'ts, 88
easiest type to handle, 88-89
environment, protecting, 94-95
land costs a factor, 87-88
leverage possibilities, 89
low investment-high return, 87
overdeveloping, avoiding, 90
proceeding, 89-90
profit, factors affecting, 87
suggestions, 91-94
topographical maps, ordering, 95-96
wholesale, buying tract, 89
Subdivision of property, effect of on value, 40
Subsidy programs, multifamily, 214-215
BMIR of 1961, 214
failures, 215
Section 236 program, 215
Sum-of-the-digits method of calculating depreciation, 151-152
Supply and demand, law of and real estate, 123

Surveying, 99-101, 111
deed, plotting, 101
expenses of, 100-101
identification, proper, 99-100
"Swinging singles" apartments, 185-186
Syndicating real estate, 158-163
developers, 162-163
investment trusts, 159-160
packagers, 162-163
private, 160-162
Sub Chapter S Corporation, 161
promoters, 162-163
public, 158-159

T

Tax advantages of cooperatives and condominiums, 187-188
Tax shelters, 152-157
and IRS guidelines, current, 154-155
leverage, 152-154
most favorable, 154
Taxes, increased, as reason for owner panic, 83
10% to your profit, adding by beautifying, 55
Tenancy in common, 115-116
Tenancy by entirety, 115
Title, certificate of, 111
Title, taking, 114-116
Title insurance, 111
Title search, 110
Tools to use in getting started, 35-38
Topographic maps as necessary tool, 35
ordering, 95-96
Transition in area, effect of on value, 40
Trust deed, 112-113
Trusts as ownership, 116
"Turnkey" method of developing projects, 216
20% below average market price, buying at, 54

U

Undeveloped property, beginning with, 34
Unimproved property, questions to ask before buying, 97-99
Uniqueness of each real estate situation, 124
United States Housing Acts of 1937, 216, 217
U.S. Geological Survey, 90

V

Vacation homes, rising price of, 23
Value, factors influencing, 40-41
Value per acre of farm real estate, change in regional, 142
Vo-Ag teachers, 135

W

Wall Street Journal, 49
Warehousing, 194-196
speculative buildings, 194-196
Warranty deed, 112
Washington, George, 75
Weekend homes, rising price of, 23
Westinghouse, 23
What to buy, 64-80
bargain situations, 65-68
best buys, 65-68
cheap property, 70-71
choices, making profitable, 72-74
farmland, 73-74
residential lots, 73
developer, selling to, 69-70
distress property, 71-72
home ownership, 74-80
advantages, 75-76
disadvantages, 76-80
mortgage, how to gain on, 79-80
opportunity, recognizing, 68
shifting, constant, of real estate, 64
sleepers, 65-68
why buy, 65
for investor, 65
for speculator, 65
Wholesale, buying tract, 89
Workmen's compensation laws, 119

Z

Zoning regulations, knowledge of as necessary tool, 35